Choice Points
Essays on the Emotional Problems
of Living with People

The MIT Press
Cambridge, Massachusetts,
and London, England

Choice Points
Essays on the Emotional Problems
of Living with People

John C. Glidewell

Set in Linotype Optima by P&M Typesetting, and printed
by Publication Press Inc. Bound in the United States of
America by The Colonial Press Inc.

Second printing, September 1972

ISBN 0 262 07038 3 (hardcover)
ISBN 0 262 57026 2 (paperback)

Library of Congress catalog card number: 71-118347

Preface

During the past twenty years of working as a social psychologist, I have been called upon from time to time to say in plain language what I think is involved in the joys and griefs of living and working closely with other people. The task has been especially challenging when I have been involved with the National Training Laboratories in undertaking to train people to use a wider range of alternatives in their quest for joy in work and joy in play and joy in love. It was important to me to try to define the problems as simply and as clearly as I could, and I made a variety of attempts to say what I thought these problems were all about.

I am a scientist by trade, but the statements certainly could not be dignified as science. The ideas were only very vaguely, if at all, substantiated by systematic empirical data. The statements were sometimes called theory, but they were not. They lacked the order and rigor of theory. I'm pretty sure no philosopher would call them philosophy. They lacked the logical integrity of philosophy. Perhaps they could be called essays. Perhaps it doesn't matter what they are called.

John C. Glidewell
Chicago
February 1970

Acknowledgments

The feelings and ideas in this work have been stimulated by many people. It is simply not possible to specify all of them. A few of them, however, deserve special mention. The basic organization of the essays was taken from the work of W. R. Bion and his conceptions of the basic assumptions of group emotionality. I first heard the words, "choice points," from Herbert A. Thelen, and much of my thinking has been stimulated by him. Warren G. Bennis encouraged my development of the concept of choice points and, indeed, the concept of choice. I first became impressed with the importance of cycles in human interaction in my collaborative work with Lorene A. Stringer. Guy E. Swanson introduced me to the conception of the constitutional arrangements underlying decision-making. The concept of reciprocity in human interaction was brought to life for me by Alvin W. Gouldner. A host of others have had important influences, too, and I regret that I often have not given credit where credit was due.

Edith W. Seashore, Warren G. Bennis, John J. Sherwood, and William J. Underwood reviewed early drafts of the manuscript with involvement and enthusiasm that were deeply appreciated. Special reviews were made by Pamela G. Lipe and Carole R. Smith. To all these friends, I offer fond appreciation.

J.C.G.

Choice Points
Essays on the Emotional Problems
of Living with People

1
On Choice Points

A Time for Choosing

For a long time I can swim along comfortably in the moving currents of the steady stream of life. Work progresses, families grow, and most of us perform our duties pretty much in accord with long-standing mutual expectations. Life isn't simple, but it is fairly regular and predictable. All of this regular part of life and work and following mutually understood expectations is, I think, tremendously important. I think that this sort of regularity is the basis of most of the sustained productivity and achievement that have built civilizations. But it is not what I want to call attention to.

I want to call attention to the irregular points—the points that begin the creation of new civilizations. The critical points in life for me are the surprising ones, points where standing expectations are violated. These are points at which choices are made, consciously or unconsciously. These are the points that set courses that change a family or change a city. Sometimes choice points come up slowly and gradually. I'm pretty sure I don't notice them until it is too late. Sometimes choice points come up suddenly and dramatically. I am startled and disturbed by the flat demands they make on me.

Faced with a choice point, I find that I am much involved emotionally. I feel all sorts of things. I seem to be scared, angry, hurt, sad, and even sometimes glad—all at once. I can pretend I have no choice, like saying that I must climb the mountain because it is there. I can try to restore the old order and way of looking at things, like saying we've got to train more old-fashioned humanitarian country doctors. I can try something new like going around without a watch just to see if time has come to mean more to me than it should. I can be just immobilized by it all, while my pulse races, and my brow sweats, and my scalp itches, and my nerves are paralyzed.

Whatever I find myself doing, I become aware that I must make a choice. I must make a choice or find the choice made for me. I must choose from whatever alternatives my experiences have stored up and from whatever alternatives my emotions make available to me. I must try to calculate the risks involved, and manage my fears while calculating.

Faced with a choice point, like whether to challenge a bully or offer him friendship, I know that my choice may expose some of my weaknesses, and I could be humiliated. I know, also, that new and more realistic learnings may become available for both me, the bully, and our fellows. And I know that, even if I am wrong in my choice, the bully, my fellows, and I could emerge better men, humbled perhaps but not humiliated.

Faced with a choice point like making a proposal of marriage, I know that it is an exciting and frightening and critical point in life. I may even see that there can be no inconsequential choice. I can be scared about making the choice, and I can be deeply grateful that I have the freedom to choose, and even be proud that my choice will have consequences. And I can still be scared to choose.

To explain some more of what I mean by choice points, let me repeat a story that was making the rounds of young parents during the late 1940s. The story had a real basis, as most stories do, and this is the basis of that story.

Just after World War II, I was one of the thousands of married veterans who found themselves students in the universities of the country. My wife, my daughter, and I lived in a cracker-box apartment, partitioned out of a former barracks building, transplanted from an abandoned army camp to a former girls' athletic field. It was an interim period of life, and we suspended many of the demands we might make on one another and on our friends. We dressed more casually (and economically), we ate more simply (and economically), and we entertained each other more spontaneously (and economically).

There were ninety families in the half-square block area where we lived, and some hundred and fifty children under ten years old. You can see that the wives almost always grasped any opportunity to get away for a short time. One Saturday my wife and a neighbor planned a day-long shopping tour. I agreed to "sit" with a pair of two-year-olds, our daughter Pam and our neighbor's son Oscar. Oscar, like a lot of other kids in that half-square block, was a fellow who met life more than halfway. His brain was as fast as light and as sharp as a needle; his body was as tough as leather and as active as a tiger cub. He entered a room like a whirlwind. Two minutes after entering, he handled, asked questions about, and tested the strength of every object and every person within his reach. We loved him and knew him well. That morning only unbreakable objects were within his reach. His mother, as she and my wife were leaving, turned in the doorway and said, "He didn't eat any breakfast at all. Try to get him to eat some lunch."

I didn't know it then, but that remark set into action a chain of choice points. I didn't recognize most of them at the time, but looking back I have never forgotten any of them. And I have looked back at them often. Let me tell you how it went.

Being a graduate student in psychology, I felt I knew a thing or two about children. In fact, I had just finished a course in child development and a lot of observations of two-year-olds. I knew that they would play, separately mostly, without much supervision. Sure enough, they did just that, requiring little from me. I just kept them in sight and congratulated myself on my good judgment and skill at minimum supervision.

Lunchtime came. I called to them sprightly, "Who would like some lunch?"

Quick as a flash, Oscar snapped back, "Not me!"

I had missed another choice point and I had made another mistake. I shifted my approach. "All right," I said, "I'll have some lunch. If you two want to join me you can." Pam watched the whole thing with fascination.

I was pretty good at heating up canned soup. I knew they both liked bean soup, and soon I had a pot of bean and bacon bubbling away. Then I remembered my textbook. The thing to do was to give Oscar some positive choices; no questions which could be answered yes or no. With that thought, I made peanut butter and jelly sandwiches. The pot of soup and the sandwiches were ready, and I asked, "Who wants soup and who wants sandwiches?"

"I don't want any lunch!" Oscar was quiet and firm.

"OK," I returned, with phony indifference.

I sat down and began to eat. Pam joined me. Perhaps she knew how desperately I needed support. Perhaps she was just hungry. Oscar played with a toy truck.

I had passed another choice point. By now I was aware how much I was on the spot. I knew my choices had consequences. In some way I didn't understand, I knew, also, that the consequences went beyond food and nutrition. Courage and cowardice, freedom and slavery, support and indifference—in some small way all of them were involved.

After a time I turned to Oscar. "Don't you like bean soup?"

"Sure. But not for lunch."

On Choice Points

"What would you like for lunch?"
Oscar's eyes sparkled with lights of mischief.
"I'd like a worm!" Oscar shouted.
"A worm?" I was shocked. He was tickled.
"A worm!" This time he shouted louder.

I was well aware by now that I was in a special kind of fight. For Oscar it was independence day. For me, it was examination day; my resourcefulness as an adult was being challenged. For Pam, it was loyalty day. She was supporting me, and she knew well how much I needed her.

"OK," I replied, "a worm." Outside we went. I rammed the spade into the ground with rare vigor, my excitement mounting. Soon I extracted a nice, long earthworm. Back into the house, a quick wash job, and the worm was on a plate before a surprised but unruffled Oscar.

"You didn't cook it."

I moved quickly. Out of the plate, into a fry pan with a little butter, and in no time the worm was earthworm sauté. Back on the plate and again in front of Oscar. He looked up at me and in unbelievable innocence, said, "Cut it up."

I moved even more quickly. I cut the worm into two pieces. I nearly growled.

"Eat."

"You eat with me."

At a time like that, at a choice point like that, even knowing my own foolishness, I could not go down in defeat. In my anger and tension, I felt sure I had only one alternative—deceit.

I picked up half the worm, pretended to eat it, and palmed it into my pocket. I did the trick pretty well. Oscar's eyes were on my mouth, pretending to chew. He never looked at my pocket. As I finished my chewing, Oscar's face clouded over, his mouth turned down and he began to cry. In between his sobs he struck the last blow.

"You ate *my* half."

That was the end of that battle. But it will never leave my memory. For me, that lunch with Pam and Oscar summed up all the dimensions of all the chains of bungled choice points that have cropped up in and around my emotional problems of living with people. They seem simple to summarize now:

When to fight and when to run away; and how to fight and how to run away; and

When to be dependent and when to be dependable; and how to be dependent and how to be dependable; and

When to offer love and when to seek love; and how to offer love and how to seek love.

Just to Define the Issues

I am going to write as if choice points really had just two alternatives. It is perfectly clear that life is not really as simple as that. It is also clear, however, that simple ideas are really the most useful ones. They can be assembled and taken apart and reassembled to fit together into many different kinds of understandings of the emotional problems of living with people.

Simple stones can be fitted together into many different kinds of complicated and beautiful structures, some for working and producing, some for playing and laughing, some for searching and learning, some for sitting and pondering, and some for kneeling and praying. In the same way, I shall try to assemble and take apart and reassemble my simple pairs of emotional alternatives to try to define and understand many different kinds of complicated and perplexing emotional problems, some for working and producing, some for playing and laughing, some for searching and learning, some for sitting and pondering, and some for kneeling and praying.

I shall try, as carefully and clearly as I can, just to define these emotional choice points, these emotional problems of living with people. I can offer no clear solutions to the problems. I really do believe that my simple summary of emotional choice points, and their two-way choices, just may be perpetual emotional problems of living together. To define the issues is task enough for me. To resolve them is too much for me. But, it has meant a lot to try carefully to think about just what is involved in these perpetual problems of living with people:

When to fight and when to run away; and how to fight and how to run away; and

When to be dependent and when to be dependable; and how to be dependent and how to be dependable; and

When to offer love and when to seek love, and how to offer love and how to seek love.

2
On Fight and Flight

On Fights and Self-respect

For a long time I thought that I, like any man, could hold onto a reasonable ambition and pursue it in peace, with my leaders and with my fellows. I thought I could share with other men whatever resources I could muster, and that I could expect other men to share with me whatever resources they could muster. I thought that we could properly share our varying resources, not equally, but equitably, each according to his own investment in our common destiny.

I thought that the particular ambitions and the particular resources I held were pretty much peculiar to me and that the particular ambitions and the particular resources each of my fellows held were pretty much peculiar to him. Men being different in ambitions and resources, they needed, I thought, to swap and trade, so that each could pursue his own ambitions even when personally he could command but few of the many resources he needed for the pursuit. He could bargain for an equity appropriate to his investment. He could swap about and exchange with others. He could use the resources of other men and they could use his. All men could swap about as their needs and desires required, and each, if he tried, could find equity, or find that his ambitions were not really reasonable, and find a way to cope with his own unreasonableness.

It was not true. I could not hold onto a reasonable ambition and pursue it in peace with my fellowman. Some injustices were too cruel. Some destruction was too evil. I saw the agonized shock of a man killed in cold-blooded routine. I saw the bloated bellies of starving infants, helpless, bewildered. I saw the bloody guts of a man ripped open with a bayonet. I saw the empty face of a mother who held the charred body of her baby, caught In the fires ot a riot of bitter hatred.

I joined some battles. Some battles were joined for me. Some of the battles were worth fighting. I left them with honor and pride. Some of the battles were not worth fighting. I left them with dishonor and shame.

The real question, I found, was not how to avoid a fight or how to keep the peace. The real question was when to fight and when to run away, and, even more crucial, how to fight and how to run away.

On Fights and Destruction

This business of getting into fights is, for me, all mixed up with very important values. They are values I set on mutual human respect and trust, freedom of individual thought and expression. I want others to be considerate of my feelings, ideas, and actions—at least as considerate as I am of theirs. I also want to be able to take criticism, even caustic criticism. I will hurt when I take it, and I will flinch, openly or inside me. After I have flinched, I will think. In time, I want to be able to make clear and reasoned judgments about the validity of the criticism I take, but I want it to be understood that any really clearheaded criticism is often acutely painful for me. I want my honest efforts to be understood, I want my strengths and weaknesses to be understood, but I don't want to make a career out of being understood.

Having thought, and believing I know what I am doing, I want to be able to fight clean and hard, with both my fellows and my leaders, for those things worth fighting for. I want to fight because the issue is important and not because I feel the urge to outsmart my fellows or discredit my leaders or just to hurt others.

It is the easiest thing in the world for me to want to hurt others. The urge to hurt comes just a split second after I have been hurt. I know that hurting other people will not make me hurt any less, but the urge to retaliate is a powerful one, an incredibly powerful one. The urge to retaliate surely must be tied to man's most primitive reflexes.

Often enough I deny to myself that I really want to hurt anybody. I maintain that my fight is quite impersonal. I fight not against a person but against some evil or for a search for some truth. It is only later that I can understand my delusion. I am fighting to hurt people.

On occasion, however, I can contain, with great effort, my urge to fight back. Once I found myself facing an investigating committee of a public body. One of my associates had, in the course of some research we were doing, committed a grievous breach of confidence. He had told some respondents that their reports were confidential and bore no identifying marks, but he had hidden a secret identification number on the forms. He was discovered. The respondents were justifiably very angry. My associate said, and I'm pretty sure it was naïvely true, that the identification was solely to be able to tell who had not turned in the report and must be reminded. Whatever the intent, it was a gross breach of confidence. And I stood before the investigating committee to account for the breach. The chairman opened the questioning.

"Is it true that you allowed identification numbers to be secreted on a confidential report?"

I felt quite vulnerable, and I was. I listened carefully to every word, and the word "allowed" bothered me. I responded.

"The numbers were in fact secreted and I was responsible."

"That, sir, is not an answer." The chairman was visibly annoyed with me. "Do not evade the question. Did you or did you not?"

"Did I what?"

"Sir, you are trying my patience. Once more, did you allow identification numbers to be secreted on a confidential report?"

"Did I allow . . ." I tapered off. My thoughts were racing. I didn't want to split hairs. The numbers were hidden on the reports. I was the supervisor of the man who hid them. I stopped it, but not soon enough. I did not supervise closely enough to know that he did it. That kind of supervision is too close for a scientist. I had to give him that freedom and live with the risk and take the responsibility.

"Yes, I allowed it."

"You admit it." The chairman was shocked.

"I allowed it," I repeated more loudly and clearly—to bolster my own courage.

"You, sir, were dishonest. You represented the reports to be confidential and you allowed identification to be hidden on them..." I interrupted him.

"I was..." He interrupted.

"Dishonest. Dishonest is what you were..."

"I..."

"You admit it. You offer no excuse, no reason. Because, sir, there is no reason. You did not care."

By now I was boiling inside, but I was sure I was being baited and I refused to rise to the bait. The trouble was I couldn't reply at all.

"I, I..." I stuttered.

"You did not care. Trusting people were tricked. I can see you laughing at the people you tricked..."

"No harm came..."

"Surely you must feel some shame. Although you certainly don't look it. Surely you can't be so unconcerned as you seem. Have you no..."

"I have made my statement." Now I found my tongue. I spoke in sharp, clipped syllables.

On Fight and Flight

"My statement was simple. I was brief. I allowed a breach of confidence . . ."

"You allowed . . ."

This time I interrupted sharply.

"I am prepared to accept the consequences of my error."

"And you will, sir. You most certainly will. Your dishonesty is a reflection on your profession, on your colleagues, and on your community."

And so it went. I took a lot of abuse, and I felt proud that I had not risen to the bait. But I was in for a surprise. Many of my colleagues were present. They gathered around me after the hearing, hurt and disappointed.

"Why," they asked, "did you let him get away with that?" "You didn't have to take that."

"Where was your backbone, Jack?"

"I never saw you buckle under to a phony like that."

"You could have tied him in knots."

I supposed I could have. I certainly felt as strong an urge to retaliate as I ever felt anywhere. At the choice point, I took another course. What had I done?

When I can look back at such a fight in a time of peace, I come to understand just how strong it is, this urge to hurt persons in retaliation. It is a human force as strong as any electromagnetic physical force. It is as strong as gravity and as difficult to circumvent. As with gravity, it is not impossible to create conditions in which the force is neutralized, but effectively to neutralize the urge to revenge requires a very tricky adjustment, an adjustment to a kind of social weightlessness. That time I had been able publicly to absorb one personally painful attack after another, and to absorb it without retaliation. But I found that my fellows had begun to wonder whether I could "carry my weight." Some sort or degree of self-esteem, it seems, has to be outwardly demonstrated as well as inwardly felt, even for the most thick-skinned of independent people. I understand better why a leader of a minority group must always look clever, strong, and fierce.

It was in the course of looking back at my fights, when I carried my weight and when I didn't, that it occurred to me that fights are always destructive, fights of all forms and all fierceness, from the friendliest disagreement to the most brutal attack. I now propose that fight always—yes, always—involves destruction of resources, be they objects, time, or human relationships. I can run away from my destructiveness by denial. I can clothe my fights with humor, sometimes with both good taste and good effect. Humor is often both good-natured and hostile at the same time. I can strike my blows as altogether appropriate and perceptive intellectual analysis, even correct intellectual analysis, of the ideas of a friend who has asked for my analysis. Both intellectual analyses of others' ideas and surgical incisions in others' bodies have a necessary component of hostility. It is how the hostility is used that is important. I can launch an attack for the protection of the weak, and find myself both charitable and vicious, depending upon who was being defended and who was being attacked. No matter what its form—humor, logical analysis, protection, personal criticism, or even that well-known "faint praise"—all these are fights. All destroy some resources to some extent. As overstated as it may sound, this is my proposition: All fights are destructive.

When my older daughter was a girl of four or five, I was on active duty in the Korean War. Once at dinner she asked me, "Do Air Force planes drop bombs on real cities?"

"In wartime they do."

"Do any people get killed?"

"Yes, some get killed." By now I was hopelessly caught in the impossible task of explaining the cruel folly of war to a trusting child.

"Why do we kill people?"

"They are our enemies. They are trying to kill us or our friends. That makes them our enemies."

"Do any little children get killed?"

"Yes, sometimes."

"Are they our enemies?"

All my adult wrappings fell off, and I stood exposed to my child in all my foolishness. I spoke through the shame in my heart and the hot tears in my eyes.

"No, they are not our enemies."

I paused to regain my composure.

"The world can be a cruel place. But I promise you that I will do all I can in my time to help build a world in which little children will be safe. It's a solemn promise."

I'll never forget the promise. But I haven't had much effect on the world in trying to keep it.

I do fight, in what I feel is righteous anger. I do fight for values I feel are worth more than peace, even more than life itself. I have, and I expect you have, in this world of wars, participated to some degree in the cruel destruction of vast numbers of human beings and of great empires of material resources, in what we firmly believed was a fight for human freedom. I fought because I believed that the end was worth the cost. I would join the fight again, if it were a fight against human slavery and for human freedom, a fight against human degradation and for human dignity, a fight against reflexive violent revenge and for reflective lawful human justice, idealistic as it may be.

I know that I would be fighting violence with violence, cruelty with cruelty, and I would sustain myself in this folly by my belief that destruction and death, including my own, is to be preferred to a life of terror. I will fight for ends that I, alone or with my fellows, judge to be worth the cost in destruction. But it is never easy to know just what I am doing. What is the dignity and freedom of man that it must be gained at the cost of the life of an innocent child? Each man knows in the back of his mind that life is temporary. In both revolution and evolution, individual lives are destroyed. Evolution is a lot slower than revolution, but no less deadly to the individual.

In a very great world war or in a very small personal conflict, I must always ask myself questions. Is it a fight for vainglory, for self-enhancement, like a fight for a delusion of self-image, like a fight for personal power for the power's sake, like a fight for pride, or like a fight against the humiliation of being weak or being wrong? Such fights involve a person's judgment about the relative worth of himself and his fellows. Often it is hard for me to tell the difference between a grasping fight for vainglory and a noble fight for human rights and dignity. Nothing is more natural than a fight for self-preservation; nothing is more hollow than a fight for self-enhancement.

Could I destroy a human being now, even in defense against attack on human liberty? Judged against mankind's long and painful search for truth about mankind and the universe, in the long run, one life is of no importance. Judged against one man's long and painful search for truth about himself and the universe, one life is the only thing that is important.

On Fights, Work, and the Worker

In the face of my concerns about fighting and its destruction, on the battlefield or in the conference room, I struggle to learn how to fight.

I find myself searching for some form of honest analysis of my work with other people. In the interest of truth and reality, we must look at our work with a clear eye. I mean public evaluation, publicly arrived at. I would not deny the need for, or the value of, informal or confidential private evaluation, even in the washroom. Sometimes it is really wise to run away. Sometimes public evaluation really can be too hot to handle, too destructive to be worth the cost. I would suggest, however, that confidential evaluation, like most forms of flight, severely limits the communication of feelings and ideas. Thereby, it also limits organizational productivity and individual learning. It distorts, more than it brings out, the raw realities of the qualities of the products. And it polishes over the rough spots of the true nature of relationships among the people.

I must ask myself, "When and how can I, as a member of a work group, criticize products, work habits, suggestions, recommendations, regulations? When can I criticize and how can I criticize without destroying what have been reasonably satisfying and productive relationships? How can I help evaluate our work without starting an irreversible process of destruction—destruction of resources like ideas and skills and feelings and honest goodwill?"

I have sat still in many work groups while we were stalled and depressed. We could not act because we could not evaluate our plans. We were immobilized in our concern about what we sincerely believed to be the inevitable personal pain and destruction that would be the price of honest evaluation. We never came right out and said so, but we did not seek information because we did not want the information. It hurt.

I, and I think most others, really believed that our product would be inadequate if we failed to criticize our work then and there. I felt that, in good conscience, we could not run away from our inadequacies, now or later. Our criticisms must somehow be made in the interest of pride in our work, individual dignity as workmen, and group self-respect. At the same time, I, and most others, really believed that honest, clear, and concise criticism would destroy more interpersonal goodwill than the product was worth. We knew the people were more important than the products, but we wanted both—competence and compassion. We sat still, nonetheless, stalled, tense, and depressed, hoping that running away would not just lead us to greater destruction later.

Once when I was new in a work group, I felt constrained to say to a most perceptive lady from Newfoundland, "I want you to understand that I intend nothing personal in the comment I want to make. It is a critical comment, but it is about your idea, not about you."

She responded to me in a voice that was altogether civil, quiet, and clear. She said, "The most important thing about me right now is my idea."

In one brief, simple sentence she brought me face to face with the reality of my own self-deception. At that point I knew, and the group knew, that we could no longer maintain the myth that we could criticize our ideas without also criticizing our people. I could see that in this work group, in any work group, it was not possible, really, if anyone was to take pride in his work, to separate the contributions from the people who made them, be they individuals, groups, or organizations. If I undertook to criticize any contribution, no matter how respectfully, calmly, or kindly I phrased it, I was going to attack any person associating himself with the contribution. It was a sobering realization, and I was paralyzed.

My discerning friend from Newfoundland, in her clear understanding, was able to help us both. "I should be most disappointed," she said, "if you do not make your criticism of my idea, but you musn't think that it won't hurt. It will, and I shall need your help and your patience— and your criticism—if I am clearly to understand what you have to say."

I then became more clearly aware that she was trying to prepare both of us for the destruction of the phony part of our relationship. The idea that we could attack and destroy ideas without affecting people was a phony idea. She was also trying to prepare us for our need for mutual support in rebuilding our ruptured relationship. We would need special support if our rebuilt relationship was to be based on more realistic understanding of the necessity for the critical evaluation of proposals.

For me, then, the issue then became: Would the fight destroy more than could be rebuilt? Could any relationship be rebuilt on a more realistic basis? Clearly we had destroyed a part of our old relationship; we could never regain it. Equally clearly, we might be able to rebuild a new relationship, more realistic, and thus more productive and less tense. With this remarkable lady from Newfoundland, the prospects for rebuilding were promising.

All of us could also see that, under other conditions with other people, the rebuilding would not be so promising; it could be even more unrealistic than what we destroyed. But the issue remained: Will the fight destroy more resources —ideas, skills, feelings, relationships, trust— than we could rebuild on a more realistic basis? When would we start an irreversible destruction? Are there human relations that, once destroyed, can never be reconstructed?

One critical incident of fight and flight stands out in my memory. I served on the board of directors of a small company. We were working from crisis to crisis, but as time passed we found somewhat longer intervals of calm between each crisis. We were surviving and growing rapidly, because we were in fact providing some excellent products. There were five of us on the board, plus the chairman. The chairman was Art. He had founded the company and, in a way, invested his life in it. The president, Ted, was a professional manager. He had only a little money invested, but his reputation for competence was at stake. Marv and Les were senior members of the board. They had made large investments, and they were deeply involved in the business. Hal and I were smaller investors who were on the board to supply professional resources, but we, too, were deeply involved.

My learning began, I think, during one routine board meeting. Ted, the president, was reporting on the great success of a new product. He paused for a second in his presentation, and Art, the chairman, interrupted him.

"I'd like to hear more about the market areas . . ."

Ted then interrupted, surprised.

"The market areas?"

"Yeah, are we going over in all the market areas? I'd guess that it might be very uneven." Art seemed to be probing for something, but I couldn't fathom what it was. I felt uncomfortable.

"Well, I don't have that information right at hand now . . ." Ted seemed upset. Art interrupted again.

"Can you get it?"

"Now?"

"Yes, now."

Ted was more upset and confused. His face was flushed.

"Well, sure. Just a minute." He left the room, and the rest of us sat in a strange sort of silence. I felt sure each of us wanted to turn to Art and ask for some sort of explanation of what he was doing, but, somehow, none of us said a word. It was a strange and tense silence.

Ted returned with a stack of papers. Without a sound he sat down and began to leaf through them. All of us watched, maintaining our strange silence. The rustle of the papers was the only sound in the room. Finally Ted slammed his hand on the table. "Dammit, I guess I can't right now. I guess I don't have that information. I'll get it for you. I'll get it for you later today.

He was looking at Art, but Art made no response.

"All right?" asked Ted.

Art spoke with quiet resignation. "All right, Ted, later today."

Again there was a strained silence. I was feeling that I could not let the incident pass without some further inquiry, but I also felt that to inquire would be to stir up something best left alone. Ted's report continued, and we completed our work routinely. I had the uneasy feeling that I had failed to act, to make a choice I could have made, at an important choice point.

Two weeks later, at the start of the next meeting, Ted asked Art, the chairman, for a suspension of the agenda to allow him to bring up a pressing problem. Art readily agreed.

"It is rather hard for me to do this, but I believe that I must for the good of the company. Art has agreed previously that I bring it up."

Ted stopped for what seemed to be a long time. He looked nervously around the room and shifted his weight in his chair. His face was flushed and his hand trembled. At last he continued.

"Art has told me privately that he believes I have withheld information from him and the board, information about failure in some markets."

All eyes turned to Art. He sat very still and, almost without moving his lips, he spoke tersely.

"That is correct."

The vein in Art's temple throbbed.

"What's correct?" This came like a shot from Marv.

"Just what Ted said."

"That he withheld . . . ," I started to try to clarify.

"That there were failures . . . ," Marv cut it.

"Wait now . . ."

"Wait . . ."

We were shouting. Somehow Les got the floor.

"Wait now," Les pleaded. "Take it easy. Let's be sure we know what we are talking about. First there is the question—uh—the question of whether or not we have had some important losses in some cities."

"We have." Art almost spat out the words. "And Ted has been lying about it." I felt my insides grow tense.

"Lying! For God's sake, Art, that's . . ." Ted had seemed scared before; now he was shocked and angry as well.

"Can you back that up?" The question came from Marv, it sounded like a pistol shot.

"No, he can't," shouted Ted. "He's just blowing off. I don't know where he got his suspicions, but they *are* suspicions, just suspicions, nothing more."

"Suspicions, no; accusations, yes. I defy you to show us the information." Art was on his feet, jabbing his finger toward Ted. "Show us!" he shouted again.

"Goddamit, quiet down. You're supposed to be grown men." Marv was exasperated and he shouted loudest of all, but he got a pause in the fight. It was Les who took advantage of the pause.

"Now, let's look at this again." His voice had a high pitch. "I'm sure Art isn't calling Ted a liar, anymore than . . ."

"I *am* saying he lied. He did." Art was sharp and clear and angry.

Les was shocked. He said, "I was trying to help you . . ."

"Help I don't need . . ."

"OK, OK." Les was bitterly irritated now. "Let's see what we can find out about this thing."

Hal tried his hand. "This unfavorable sales information is known to Ted, but he is keeping it from us, according to Art." Hal was still tense and struggling to be very clear. But to Art it was a ploy. It sharpened his anger.

"I was clear enough the first time. You understood me." Art was giving no quarter.

"Now wait again. Wait." Les was sorely disturbed. "Let's call a cease-fire. We're getting nowhere this way. Let's come back to this later."

"Yeah, back to the agenda." Hal was ready to leave the fray. But I was not. It had not been a very clean fight, and I didn't want another one like it, but I could feel an important choice point slipping way. As scared as I was, I could not turn away this time.

"Not yet," I said, "not just yet."

"What the hell, Jack . . ." Les was annoyed with me. "You want to stir up . . ."

"I want to *clear* up," I interrupted. "I think we can clear the thing up. I think we can really find out. About those market reports." I was scared, my pulse was racing and my scalp was itching, but I really meant it. I was sure we could not afford to run away from this issue.

"Yeah." It was Art. He spoke quietly now and we were reassured. "No name-calling, Ted, but now can we see those market reports?"

Ted was quiet. All of us waited coldly for his reply.

"Ted, do you have them?" I asked.

"Well, in fact—right now—I don't. Right now. But . . ."

"But!" Art shouted again. "But what?"

Les moved an open hand toward Art. "Please, Art . . ."

"It's been weeks since I first asked . . ."

"Let him explain," I asked.

"I'd like to hear what he has to say," Hal added.

"So would I," Art returned, acidly now.

"Some of the reports were delayed. I called the men in the field. Their reports should be here today." Ted spoke quite deliberately, but I felt there was a tone of disgust in his voice, disgust that his explanation was even necessary.

Marv looked puzzled. "They were delayed?"

"Yes, for some time. A few weeks." Ted now spoke in a surprisingly matter-of-fact way.

"Ted," I made a bid for his attention. "There is something missing somehow. You reported the total figures. Did you estimate the delayed reports?" Now I was suspicious, too.

"There really *is* something missing, Ted." Art was mounting his attack again. "You are not telling us something."

"I don't know what that would be," Ted said nervously, now much on the defensive.

"Now, Ted, just tell us how you put together the total figures. There are all sorts of ways you could have done it, legit, without the delayed reports." This was from Les.

"Oh, sure. Well, I guess I didn't make the whole thing clear. You see, I did estimate on the basis for the first reports . . ."

"First reports!" Art struck out. "What first reports?"

"Well, the first reports did have some errors.

I sent them back for correction." Ted was tense and shaking now.

"You sent them back! They weren't delayed. You haven't felt it was necessary to mention that? Until now?" Art was on his feet again, shouting.

"The reports with the errors, they were not favorable, they showed no sales, right?" This was from Marv. His tone was quiet. There was a sense of despair in the room.

"Not all of them. Some were very favorable."

"How many?" asked Hal.

"Some."

"How many, dammit?" shouted Art.

"We blew it in a few cities!" Ted shouted back. There was a long silence.

"How many?" asked Hal again quietly.

"I don't know, I don't know." Ted was now quietly desperate. "There were errors. I couldn't tell for sure. I wanted to wait until I was sure. Wouldn't you?"

"You really were covering up." I spoke quietly and sadly.

"I guess I was." Ted had now just about collapsed. "I guess I was."

All of us seemed to feel a strange combination of elation and grief. It was as if a weight had been lifted from us, and it was as if we had lost something we needed badly, confidence in Ted, but more, much more, confidence in ourselves.

There was a knock on the door. I discovered that the delayed reports were being brought in. It was a welcome interruption.

On Fight and Flight

"Here now," said Art with some excitement, perhaps a little forced. "Let's go over these and see if we can find out why we failed in those cities."

The shift brought relief, but it seemed too sudden. I was still in the aftermath of the fight, and I still wanted to get something more from it, some firmer base for us. But I still couldn't think of any way to work on the problem of trust by just talking about it.

We gathered around Art, all trying to look at the papers at once. Ted remained in his chair for a few minutes, then he rose and started toward the door. Art looked up from the reports and called to him.

"Ted, we need you." It was clear that he meant it.

"Me?"

"You. We have work to do. And now we have a basis for doing it. You still know more about what's behind these figures than any of us." He paused and reached out his hand toward Ted.

"And now we have a better access to what you know."

It was a great move, and we were back to work more soberly. I was sure we really did have better access to what Ted knew. I was also sure that the wounds were still open, raw, and tender. All of us had doubts about Ted. He had lied to us once. What did we know about whether he would lie to us again?

We had trusted Ted so completely. And he had

lied to us. If he could lie, anybody could lie. Each of us was sneaking glances at the others. Our old trust was gone. It had been phony. To build a new one, we would have to gamble.

The compelling force was that all of us knew that the fight had been vitally necessary. It had been hard to admit that the old sense of trust was phony, but the fight had made that clear. Somehow we had to find a way to build a new trust based upon a more nearly true access to the knowledge about the weaknesses all of us had—the fears and the antagonisms and the cover that each of us could develop. We had a better chance to fight a cleaner, more open, working fight the next time; the next time we had to seek out more honestly some painful truth about ourselves and our work.

It was a gamble, but we had now more knowledge and therefore more strengths to add to our resources. Maybe experience, painful experience as well as joyful experience, is the only soil in which realistic human trust can put down its roots.

We would have to trust even when we were scared that we could not afford to. I discovered a critical key to human trust. It was easy to trust a man who had always been trustworthy. The great task was to trust a man who had not been trustworthy. As naïve as it sounds, I guess such a gamble is really required if men are ever to rebuild what they destroy in a fight, if men are ever to learn from the scars of truth.

On a License to Level

Many times my leaders and my fellows have said to me, quite soberly, that to work well, we must "level with each other." They understood, and said, that to level with each other, we must learn to cope with the emotions which would necessarily be involved—warm, tender feelings and cold, hostile feelings. They felt that to cope with the hostile feelings involved, we must be ready to stand up under a constant cycle of destruction and reconstruction. We must live in a constant cycle: first of aggressive, working excitement; then of sober, unflinching analysis.

This seemed to me to be a fair and realistic approach to work and an honest and proper way to fight. I was ready to subscribe to it. I believed I was ready to express quite frankly the real ideas and feelings that I experienced inside me. It was a contract to be mutually honest, and I was fully ready to support honesty.

All of us, I still believe, were asking for frankly expressed truth—truth in the sense that we would express truthfully the ideas and feelings we really experienced then and there. The ideas themselves may have been invalid, the feelings may have been impulsive, but they were just exactly what we thought and felt, not just what we believed would be "good for the group" or what we believed others wanted to hear. All of us, I still believe, were scared, too, because we really meant what we were saying.

We felt that we surely must not lie, but we

found ourselves with agonizing conflicts. In the past, we had always sifted carefully what we had to say, sometimes in the interest of work, sometimes in the interest of human kindness, and sometimes in the interest of the survival of the individual or the survival of a group or an organization that we believed to be worthy.

We tried to level with one another; we tried as hard as anybody ever did, and, sure enough, we found that we really could express something of our hitherto withheld ideas and feelings. There were times when we could sharply and simply criticize the boss. There were times when we could clearly and concisely criticize our fellows. We could express the parts of our ideas and feelings we were most sure of—sure that we could say it clearly, sure that others could hear it clearly, sure that the task demanded it, sure that the boss could cope with it.

But there was much that we never could say. Some ideas remained unspoken because we were pretty sure they could not be stated clearly, because of our own conflicts about them. Some could not be heard clearly. No one of us was so strong that he could hear the true sound of everything that others thought about him. Some ideas and feelings we never could express because they could not be used. All of us had, at times, heard strongly and clearly about our self-defensive, self-maintaining habits. They unsettled us, and, in our search for peace of mind, we forgot them in spite of ourselves. As much as we wanted to, as hard as we tried to, we were still unable to change.

Many ideas and feelings we did not express because we could not be sure just what it was that we thought and felt. We could not be sure, because what we thought and felt was as much about us as it was about others. Sometimes it was more about us than it was about others. We felt that we were seeing and feeling in others what was not really in them but in us.

It was then that we thought we were cowards. We knew all sorts of ideas and feelings remained unexpressed. To be sure, they were hard to hear, hard to use, or just unrealistic, but the ideas and feelings were really there, and they were unexpressed. To cover them up, we believed, was to be dishonest, and we could not tolerate our dishonesty.

It was then that we broke loose from our restraints. We experienced the great electric excitement of spontaneous expression, and we experienced the pain and confusion of personal attack and counterattack. We tightened our grasp on our courage and fought the good fight. We tried to be responsible, too. When there was a lull in the battle, we looked bravely—well, as bravely as we could—at the consequences of what we had done. It was then that we felt the awful, empty, impotent guilt, despair, and grief that comes when one has lost his friends. "What," we asked, "is the true meaning of honest expression? What is this agreement to level with one another? Is it just a hunting license? What could be rebuilt from the destruction we had wrought?"

It was then that we ran away. We denied the validity of our experience. We "took back" our hostile statements. We cried out that we did not mean what we had said, had felt, had expressed, under this license to level. We never could, however, convince each other, or ourselves. We had, we really had, truly expressed and truly felt all those jealousies, antagonisms, and hostilities that we had always suspected lay below the surface of all our working groups. No matter how distorted by a person's self-defense, no matter how confused the expression, no matter how capricious the emotions, there they were—the awful spontaneous expression of what we really felt and thought.

It was clear to all of us that we must find out just how productive we could be under the terms of this license to level. Was it really possible for us to work effectively with others in what seemed to be a climate of mutual hostility? Under the compelling drive to recover from our wounds, we returned again to work. Each of us said, "I shall try as hard as I can to rebuild new relationships without denying what I have learned of our true feelings about each other. I shall seek a new relationship based upon the reality of what all of us have learned about our antagonisms—a relationship more realistic, more honest. I shall seek a relationship more likely to survive a continuing conflict of interest and a further frank expression of the realities of our feelings, more likely to produce honestly examined work, and, thus, more really useful and valuable work."

It was greatly reassuring to discover that it was possible to lick our wounds and, at the same time, to reestablish our small war in special and ingenious ways, so that we would not be wounded again and again in the same place. It was encouraging to see that the wounds really would heal, even while other wounds were being inflicted in our little war, to be licked and to heal, each in its turn. New expectations developed. We experienced a welcome rearousal of our self-esteem as we discovered that we could survive and grow in strength in a climate in which honestly felt hostility was not denied. We felt the special comradeship that comes from the shared survival of a common crisis. We grew in strength and confidence. An attack that once was felt as a staggering blow now was felt as a tolerable injury. We still felt real pain, but perhaps with the kind of tolerance for pain that comes to most women in childbirth, the pain that can be a part of creativity. For some men, creativity at work can be as painful as childbirth is for women, and, for some rare men, the labor can be as pain-free as with some rare women.

Along with the reassurance, there was also, sometimes, despair and grief. Not all the wounds would heal. Not all of the newly reestablished little wars prevented our being wounded again in the same place. Some relationships could not be rebuilt. Some of the destruction of our small war was irreversible.

A few of us found that a friend had been lost forever. A few of us found that we must stay and work, but we must rebuild stronger and stronger personal defenses and greater and greater inhibitions. Otherwise, our fellows would again and again be insulting our old wounds. The new defenses were more rigid and more brittle. A few of the new relationships with the group were but phony ceremonies to satisfy the need for membership. For these few, realities were denied. Relief was found in the disguise of humor. Most of us cooperated with these few unfortunate fellows. Comfort was sought in unreal escapes into polite compliments and empty ceremonials. By such inhibitions, the true resources of each of those few people were held inaccessible to the individual himself, to the group, and to the organization—even, if you will, to the civilization. We said it was a loss we had to take.

My boss, my fellows, and I, all of us, know now, from our experiences, that the license to level had become an injunction. The demand had become too fixed and rigid, too inclusive of all individuals—all individuals whose unique individuality we believed we valued highly. All of us knew that the license to level could not be an injunction. It could not be established by rules and laws. Every man ought to be equal under rules and laws. Every man must be different in his expression of his quest for truth about himself and his response to the millions of different kinds of expressions of the same quest by his leaders and his follows. Every social organization must tolerate, or even create, an enormously wide range of alternative ways and times for a man to fight for what he believes to be real and true, and to run away from what he believes to be inhumane destruction.

On Cycles: Work and Fight; Work and Flight

I am impressed by the cycles in life. The orbits of the earth and the moon, the day and the night, the winter and the summer, breathing in and breathing out, working hard and playing hard, throbbing passion and quiet tenderness.

I am pretty sure that learning moves in cycles. If one time I am eager and the rate of learning is fast, the next time I relax a bit and the rate of learning is slower. Then I bear down again and use my resources. I mobilize my ideas and skills and feelings to increase my rate of learning, only to relax again and rebuild my resources, especially my feelings. If my fellows and my bosses apply pressure, the cycle changes. The rate and the tensions stay high longer before the cycle swings, but swing it does. The cycle, I think, is the natural state of affairs.

For men at work, some cycles are the shifts from work to play, from fight to flight, from joy to despair. All of them are emotional resources used in the quest for truth.

Work, I think, is a managed fight and a managed flight. It is also a thing of cycles. A craftsman carves, then stops and looks. He looks and finds joy and pride; he looks and finds despair and pain. As it is with the craftsman, so it is with the engineer and salesman and lawyer and physician. He sees in his work either what he seeks or what he fears. He can resume his work with intensity and obsession, not daring to stop again to look at the work or to think about the meaning of it. He is too afraid that he will not find what he seeks or that he will find what he fears. He can do other things, too. He can flee from his work on the faith that on his return he will be better prepared to look and to see what his eyes behold.

He can also pace his work more carefully: from thought to action, to observation, to reflection, and back to action. He must always be alert to the choice points: when to stop thinking and start acting; when to stop acting and start thinking. When and how.

It is easy, and it is true, to say that sometimes it is as foolish to work as it is foolish to fight. No competent soldier attacks against any odds. A quick retreat from a king cobra is no act of cowardice. A vain destruction of resources is a service to no cause at all. Only the very rare, the most deeply inspired, are creative martyrs. Nothing is more tragic and wasteful than a blind, irrational, self-destructive attack. Nothing is more tragic and empty than a man who has lost his self-respect because he quailed at destruction and failed to fight for what he believed in. In the same way, nothing is more tragic and empty than a man who has exhausted himself in compulsive work because he quailed at the destruction involved in thinking about the meaning of what he was doing.

I've done some driving work in my time, even as I understood that work is aggressive. Work is aggressive because it changes things, destroys them, and constructs them. Work makes growth. The destruction of one thing and the construction of another create growth in plants and animals and men: the ideas, skills, and feelings of men. Work is aggressive because it requires evaluation of products, and negative evaluation tears down. Work is also joyful, also because it requires evaluation of its products, and positive evaluation builds up. Perhaps it takes both tearing down and building up to yield growth and joy and pride in one's work and its products.

For me and my fellows, just the same, any long-sustained grip on work and reality is a tense and exhausting task. A little relief from the tension here and there will yield a profit in long-range stamina. A fellow, a group, even a large organization, needs a break now and then. A coffee break, an afternoon recess, a square dance, a picnic, a songfest, a well-timed joke, a time and place for quiet reflection—all of these can be

wise investments in cycling which yield profits
in creative work and individual learning. A light
touch of flight in and around the work on a
serious problem can fortify people like me to
tackle what they would otherwise avoid. Running away can be a more creative act than an
obsessive, repetitive, losing battle with an old
problem. The trick is to know when and how to
run away. The cycles vary with the problems,
the people, and the processes of interchange.

A great flight is a thing of wonder and fulfillment. To leave the fray in the hands of competent fellows, to find free joy in play and laugh-
ter, to know the open action of mind and
muscle, to gain new strength in the renewal of
love, to discover new perspective from a temporary safety—to find all of these recreations requires experience and faith and skill. It is an
exciting thing for me to reach for the experience,
to nurture the faith, and to develop the skill.

The quest for joy at play isn't given very much
attention. To escape with an obsessive abandon
is as easy—and as empty—as to work with
obsessive compulsion. I can remember a time
when I went to the movies every night, so that
I would not have to confront the sterility of the
life I was living.

The faith and the fortitude I need to play well
come to me from the experience of true recreation, from a flight that really did restore and
refine my resources: my motives, my courage,
my skills, my perspectives. I can remember mak-

ing up raucous songs during a forced march of
exhausted and frightened men, and I can remember the mutual support it gave us. I can
remember my family's mood at a quiet lodge in
the deep color of an autumn afternoon and the
peaceful perspective it gave us.

The experience is not really so hard to come by,
but I have found it hard to take the time. There
is so much to be done. There really is. And even
in the last third of my life I am impatient. All of
us know how to do much more than we do,
to create justice and truth and love. A lot of
thought and action and reflection is needed fast
in this fast-moving world. How can I take the
time to play?

That's another question I know a little about,
but I don't act as if I do. I know that the work
will get done, the good fight will get fought, and
better, if I take the time to play. I must have the
faith to take the risk to run away. The experience
I need to nurture the faith and fortitude must
come from a provisional try—a small one at first,
with not too much at stake. As my investment in
flight pays returns in restored resources, my faith
and fortitude grow, my experience is extended,
and my skill develops. I have much to learn of
the great art of flight, and I am only just gaining
the faith to learn it.

To let go one's flying thoughts and surging
feelings in active, expressive play in the surf, on
the fields, down the mountains, up the streams
—all these can be rare treasures. To find diver-

sion in the expression of one's skills and feelings on a canvas, on a chessboard, on a stage, at a piano, in a yarn, all these can be great creative moments. To entertain one another—an art so much needed and so much perverted by us all —to provide for each other a real joy in play, conversation, storytelling, singing, and sharing of the wonderful and the ridiculous in everything we do, day by day: all these are parts of a great art, greater, even at its simplest, than all the great talents of commercial entertainment.

On the Quest for Truth

To ask when to fight and when to run away is to ask one to consider and reconsider how fight and flight are all mixed up with all of human affairs: ambition, both reasonable and unreasonable; respect for human values, both practical and idealistic; evaluation of products, both careful and caustic; work, both creative and compulsive; self-esteem, both vain and humble; human tension and its release, both capricious and constructive; conservation, both hoarding and nurturing; cycles of life, both balanced with poise and strained with distention; ruptured human relationships, both those to be forever lost and those to be more honestly found; human dignity, both destroyed by the human urge to hurt and constructed by the human quest for truth. All of it is human life, that one great irreversible process, that one resource which, once destroyed, is lost forever.

I think I know better now what human fight

and flight are all about. But the questions remain: When to fight and when to run away, and how to fight and how to run away? I must learn a little more about the questions each day, but I must understand that I shall die before I know very much about them. The questions are the mainsprings of the human quest for truth. The quest never ends.

3
On Dependency and Dependability

On Freedom and Resources

Some feelings have been worked into me much too well. To be regularly dependent upon others is to be weak and entrapped. To conform regularly to the expectations of others is to be weak and enslaved. That's how I feel. In my head, I know better. I know that to be dependent is sometimes to be altogether sensible, sensible enough to have good use of resources that I couldn't otherwise have. I know that to conform is sometimes to be wonderfully dependable, dependable enough to have the respect of others who are important to me. I know these things, but I don't feel as if I do or act as if I do.

In my time, and I think in most times past, people like me have been endlessly preoccupied about the freedom of man. I want to be free to shape my own destiny from my own resources, to fight my fights, to mount my flights, to find my loves, to live my own life. I try hard to shape my own destiny freely and independently from my own resources, but I find again and again that I can't. I find myself in tight conflicts. The conflicts arise with other men. My own freedom conflicts with the freedom of other men.

The freedom of mankind is, to me, a truly wondrous idea. Its accomplishment would be so great, so enabling to so many people. Even its pursuit is so honorable that it can excite me like nothing else—well, almost like nothing else. I have discovered, just the same, that the goal of the freedom of man is so honorable and so ex-

On Dependency and Dependability

citing and so unassailable that it can be a snare and a delusion.

It seems to me that freedom has been shouted out as the goal of most of the cruel and destructive little fights to which men have tried to recruit me. It has been shouted out as the goal of most of the bloody riots and butchering rebellions of the history I know.

In the bright light of morning, I have heard the rebels' call to attention, I have seen the match put to the fuel of the common spirit of enslaved men, I have felt the electric charge of loyalty to the cause of freedom, I have tasted the glory of a fierce commitment unto death. In the dull dark of night, I have heard the screams of men who died to give another man power, I have seen the shock on the faces of men who had just found that they had traded one form of slavery for another, I have felt the pain of the idealist watching a firing squad, I have tasted the bitter despair of a man who followed a fight for freedom into a jungle of beasts.

Freedom from tyranny has too many, far too many, meanings for me. Freedom, I'm sure, doesn't mean just doing what I want to do. I'm sure it doesn't mean just not having anybody telling me what to do. I'm sure it doesn't mean just being able to tell other people what to do.

Perhaps it means some kind of self-sufficient independence. It's hard to see any freedom in abject poverty. Perhaps freedom means having enough resources under my control that others can influence me no more than they should *and* having no more resources under my control than would allow me to influence them any more than I should. But I don't know how much influence there should be—in either direction. Freedom and the availability of resources get confused.

The lone trapper in the mountains is wonderfully free. He is free from dependency on others and from coercion by others. He is also sorely limited. The only resources available to him are those that he can develop himself. If he has the judgment and the skills, he can develop for himself quite enough food, clothing, and shelter, and he can deeply enjoy the rare and unspoiled beauty that nature provides for all of us who will stop to look. His resources are very limited, though. They are limited by his own interests, aptitudes, and sensitivity to beauty. Nature is not only a dramatic artist and a productive farmer, she is also a demanding mother and a tyrannical caretaker. In her domain, only the fittest survive. The lone trapper in the mountains is wonderfully free. He is also narrowly limited and sorely dependent upon the acts of nature.

An inmate in a modern prison has more resources available to him than the lonely trapper. He can enjoy a wider variety of food. He can be better sheltered from a blizzard. He can enjoy all the entertainment and beauty that the varied talents of his fellow inmates can produce. He has available to him—under conditions no more onerous than many—most of the talents, ideas, skills, and feelings of quite a heterogeneous group of people. He has all sorts of resources available, and he is imprisoned and degraded. What is freedom? The rich are not free. I know that. The poor are not free. I know that, too. Yet, I know that resources and freedom are connected. To be free is to have resources available when I need them, more resources than I can supply for myself. Resources from others ought to be paid for; something must be given in exchange. Perhaps to be free is to have resources available when I need them, and at a fair price.

On a Hundred Million Resources

My conflicts, I feel sure, are partly caused by the complexity of the civilization I live in. It seems clear to me that all of us really do want to have more resources available to us than we can possibly develop ourselves and that the organization of so very many special resources is incredibly complex. I shall have a lot to say about resources, so I want to make clear what I mean by resources. There are so many different kinds of special resources that they are hard to think about. They vary widely with men and time and place. It has helped me to think about resources as objects and skills and ideals and feelings. Yes, feelings, too, are resources, I think.

There are objects: things like garbage grinders in the sink; like a bell in a village church; like grain and meat in the storehouses of communities; like iron ore and coal in the factories of cities; and like rockets and space ships with which people try to free themselves from their dependency on the tyranny of nature.

There are skills: like the speed and precision of the surgeon's hands; like Churchill's magnificent articulation of both the dauntless courage and the gaunt fear of a whole nation; like the rare communication skill of an illiterate jungle drummer; like the thousand-mile navigational skills of a Polynesian sailor with only the feel of the wind on his cheek, the measured splash of the waves on the canoe, and the unaided eye to judge the moving stars; and like the skill of the housewife judging the proper consistency of her pancake batter.

There are ideas: like the idea of individual freedom to find one's own way of life; like the idea that people always resist changes in their way of life; like the idea that change itself, or growth itself, is progress; like the idea that there is only one God; like the idea that one race is superior to another; like the idea that all the forms of life evolved from earlier, less adaptive forms of life just by being able to survive; like the idea that war will be with us always; and like the idea that brown-shelled eggs are more nutritious than white-shelled eggs.

There are feelings: like the fear that being dependent upon others is a sign of weakness; like the joy in a child's excited gasp of recognition of a homecoming parent; like the relentless hostility of a black adolescent "growing up absurd"

On Dependency and Dependability

in the dirty streets of an alien city slum; like the love and warmth of a mother and an infant anywhere, or at least anywhere they know they can find the means for survival; like the shocked grief, the instinctive sobs, and the sober mourning of a nation that had witnessed the senseless assassination of its bright young leader; like the competently directed, driving brutality of the professional soldier who has just lost a close friend in battle; like the wondrous affection of the young lover who has just found his love returned; and like the measured fear of an experienced animal trainer in the cage with his beasts.

There are a hundred million resources: objects, plants, animals, persons—and of the persons especially, their skills and their ideas and their feelings. None of us can develop very many of these resources alone. Our complex civilization with its hundred million resources really does require specialization. I can develop those resources that I can develop best, those resources for which I have aptitudes, interests, and opportunities. I must leave it to others to develop those resources for which they have aptitudes, interests, and opportunities.

It is important to me to remember all the resources. Objects and animals and inventions and hardware are resources, but there are more. Motives and feelings and ideas and skills are resources, too. For a long time the control of food, shelter, and especially weapons was the basis of power and freedom. I look at wars that can't be won or lost or stopped. I look at youth who can see that so much is possible and so little is done. I look at statesmen who know what fools wise men can be. I wonder how so much competence and power can avail so little. I know, then, that we are coming upon a new time when the control of motives and feelings and ideas will be the new basis of power and freedom. The time is almost now.

On Mutual Dependency

In trying to understand freedom and poverty and tyranny and affluence, it has been a little helpful to me to think about the nature of social organization. Social organization requires commitments to others, and from others. Each man puts into the organization some motives, feelings, ideas, and skills. He gets out of the organization other motives, feelings, ideas, and skills, at the times and in the places and in the manner they can be used. The time and place and the manner have to be reasonably certain, and that requires commitments to others and from others. It requires dependability. If the motives, feelings, ideas, and skills involved in the give-and-take have meaning and importance, the organization can give a fellow a growing sense of worth and competence and the kind of freedom that comes with power to control many resources to secure and enrich one's life. If the motives, feelings, ideas, and skills involved are dull and trivial, the organization can give a fel-

On Dependency and Dependability

low a growing sense of worthlessness and impatience and the kind of slavery that comes with feeling the yoke of unjust control of one's life.

Man can and does construct social organizations that imprison him. He constructs not just prisons but also communities, factories, banks, and even "little leagues" of children's baseball teams. All of them can imprison a man.

I keep repeating to myself that any civilization requires specialization and organization and discipline. It requires specialization because we want to have available to each of us many more resources than any one of us can develop alone. It requires organization because we want to know when and where and how all of the specialized resources of others are to be made available to us; and we want to know when and where and how we are to make our specialized resources available to others. It requires discipline because, when we are so much dependent upon others for resources, we want to be as sure as we can be that they are dependable.

For me, freedom cannot be limiting my needs to the resources within myself. Compared to what is possible, that would be loneliness and poverty. Freedom cannot mean having no responsibilities to others. Compared to what is possible, that would be loneliness and uselessness. It just may be that my freedom is being dependent upon others because they are dependable to me and my significance is being dependable to others because they are dependent upon me. Others' freedom is being dependent on me because I am dependable to them, and others' significance is being dependable to me because I am dependent upon them. Maybe this is it: freedom is being dependent and significance is being dependable.

But that is not all of it. There are some things we must do for ourselves. There are some skills and ideas and feelings which are so much at the core of any life that all of us must develop our own. The problem becomes more complicated. What resources are to be basic and general? What resources are to be my choice and specific to my own talents? What are the minimum general resources that every one of us must develop? Physical fitness? Child rearing? Praying? Talking—talking simply and clearly? Or just expressing ourselves: our skills, our ideas, our feelings?

What resources should be left to be developed by specialists only? Gymnastics? Pediatrics? Ministering? Public speaking? Perhaps the question becomes more clear, and harder to answer, if one asks how much pediatrics should a parent know and how much should he leave to the pediatrician? How much teaching of his children should a parent do and how much should he leave to the professional educator? How much of a minister should a person be to himself and how much should he seek of the professional minister?

Call it *inter*dependency, if you want to, but the

On Dependency and Dependability

word makes it no less true that we must be quite dependent on the engineer and the teacher of reading as well as on the surgeon. We simply cannot do for ourselves and our children what they can do for us and our children. To me, this means we must be dependent. The fact that all of us are interdependent doesn't change the fact of any one man's dependency or take away any of the honor of being realistically dependent.

There was a time in the early 'fifties when I surrendered to the demands of my children and my neighbors and bought a television set. Having made it available, I haughtily ignored it the first night, for all of half an hour. I found myself sitting before it, at first curious, then fascinated, and then hopelessly hypnotized. The thing was unbelievable.

I'm sure you know that the time came when something in the silly box broke or blew out or came loose or whatever. The thing wouldn't show pictures any more. I faced the task of getting it repaired.

I had read in the papers about the television repair racket and the legal exploitation available to television repairmen. I never felt more dependent on what promised to be an undependable specialist. My dependency was an inescapable fact, and I had to cope.

From the Yellow Pages I selected a nearby repairman. I called the Better Business Bureau, always a dependable resource. They told me they had had no complaints about this one, but,

as always, they couldn't endorse anyone; anyway, he was new in the business. Almost everybody was.

I called him. Even with all my doubts and suspicions, I called him. He came, about when he said
he would. He unplugged the set, took off the
back, and tapped on the tubes with a screwdriver. He looked up at me, trying out my stern-
est surveillance, and said, "You need two new
tubes."

"Two new tubes," I parroted in my suspicious
anxiety. "How do you know?"

"Oh," he said, "you interested in electronics?"
I mumbled. I was now embarrassed. "No, not
really. I just couldn't see how you could tell that
a tube is bad by tapping on it with a screwdriver." Having expressed both my doubts and
my ignorance, I had become even more aware
of my position. I must either relax and risk my
dependency on this repairman or I must learn
enough to repair the set myself. I have neither
the interest nor the aptitude to learn electronics.
I would make a poor and inept TV repairman. To
develop the resources myself would be uneco-
nomic and even foolish. I could invest my time
to much greater advantage. Clearly, it was a time
to be dependent. He put in the tubes. I paid.

My repairman was less academic than I. He
said, "I guarantee my work for a reasonable
length of time. You can see that your set works
now; it didn't work before. I must warn you,
though," he said, "those same tubes will need to

On Dependency and Dependability

be replaced again about every six months. It's the way your set is made. Those two tubes are overloaded. I can't rebuild the set."

Sure enough, just as he said, six months later the same tubes went bad. There was no way to be sure whether the correct prediction meant competence or built-in obsolescence. This time, however, the repairman showed me how to remove all the tubes and told me how to test them on a gadget at the corner drugstore. I could make these replacements without calling him. To me, this was great. There really were some things I could do myself, as inept as I was; I did not have to depend on him for everything. And, sure enough, my wife did learn how to replace those tubes.

I am sure you know that there came a time when our repairman told us he could not repair the set in our home; he must take it to his shop. He saw my anxious look. I thought he didn't see the suspicions behind the anxiety because he said, "You can come down to the shop and see your set if you want to. We have regular visiting hours in the evening."

It is always a little easier for me to depend on a man with a sense of humor. Come to think of it, maybe he did see the suspicions behind my anxiety.

In time, the television repairmen formed an association that undertook to guarantee its members' work and to discipline or reject its less scrupulous members. The experts were organizing and disciplining themselves. It is now a lot easier for me to be dependent on our TV repairman—a specialized, organized, disciplined expert; he is dependable. I still don't understand how you can tell a tube is bad by tapping on it with a screwdriver.

I do understand better now that everybody is dependent.

On Specialists and Generalists

In the calm of everyday affairs at work and at home, I have felt much concerned and much in conflict about when to be dependent and how to be dependent. There are a lot of important choice points in routine situations. They are more deliberate and less urgent, more generalized and less specialized, but they are no less important.

How dependent should I be on the teacher of my child? She teaches my child to read. It is not a crisis. The teaching and the learning are slow and irregular. The emergency kind of dependency is clearly not appropriate.

I know that nowadays the teaching of reading is a technical and specialized task. The technical and special teaching skill is not expected of me. It is not really very suitable to my temperament and my aptitudes. Some dependency on special professional skill is appropriate.

I also remember that it was once the responsibility of parents alone to teach their children to read, when not very much was known about the ways in which learning to read can become

On Dependency and Dependability

a special problem. Now that more is known, but only to specialists, it is not clear just what a parent's responsibility is. Or is it that the special problems were caused by the specialists?

I was once very well acquainted with Dick and Jane and their dog Spot.

"See Spot run.
Run, Spot, run.
See Dick run.
Run, Dick, run.
See Jane—uh—r-r—what's that word, Daddy?"
Then there was a long silence while Daddy tried to fathom the unfathomable.

"Haven't you seen that word before?
"Oh . . . ? I don't know. Where?"
"Where?" I shouted, but how could you cope with that question?

The tears came then, and the grief and the guilt. And I knew that there was more at stake there than reading.

I know enough, and have skill enough, to do some things. I can watch with interest while my child practices reading. I can offer support and I can offer understanding, understanding that learning to read is a hard job. I can make some corrections of mistakes, especially when they are asked for by my child.

I do not know enough to be sure about when and how to correct mistakes without promoting more upset feelings than learning. I do not know enough to manage my own tensions when my child's reading does not go well. I do not know enough to be sure about the causes of any troubles in recognizing and remembering words. What I do not know can make me feel miserable when I try to help my child learn to read.

I know that the state licenses teachers. An elected board of citizens sets the standards for the selection of teachers. A professionally experienced administrator selects teachers. I know that most eager young teachers can do with competence what parents can do only with luck. I know that most young teachers have been well trained, and thoroughly indoctrinated, to know and do what I do not know and cannot do. I also know that some eager young teachers can complicate and cripple what would otherwise be a simple process of learning to read. What I know about teachers can make me feel confident, and it can make me feel scared.

How much is special and how much is general? How much is professional practice and how much is do-it-yourself good citizenship? How much can I trust the professional specialization to be sound and effective? When am I to be dependent upon the teacher and when am I to be dependable to my child? How am I to be honorably dependent upon the teacher and how am I to be honorably dependable to my child?

On Mutual Dependency and Reciprocity

All along in my thinking I have been trying to understand specialization and complementary resource development. There is another aspect of dependency and dependability. It is the ques-

On Dependency and Dependability

tion of what I am willing to pay for the resources of others. I have learned that reciprocity is involved. Some kind of equity, not equality, in the interchange of resources may be a necessary condition for an honorable dependency and dependability.

The equity can involve material resources and their symbol, money. The equity can also involve ideas and skills and feelings. It just may be that human interchange simply cannot include objects only. It seems likely that the bargain must always include ideas and skills and feelings, in addition to any objects exchanged.

The interchange of feelings is very different from the interchange of objects. Give your friend an object and you don't have it any more. You can't use it any more. Give your friend an idea or a feeling and you haven't lost it. You still have it, often with greater understanding and control of it. Perhaps you see with greater clarity what feelings are yours, what ideas are yours, and what are his. Perhaps, but probably not.

Surely anger and fear and love don't belong to anybody and do belong to everybody. But a particular anger, directed at a particular person in a particular way at a particular time and place—that was produced by me. In trying to know myself better, it has become important to me to know the difference between the particular feeling I feel and the particular feeling you feel, even if both are anger or fear or joy.

It has also become important to me to know

the part you play in the ideas I develop. It has become important to recognize the skills and ideas and feelings coming from you and how they influence the skills and ideas and feelings coming from me. As important as both of them are—yours and mine—unless I can tell the difference, I can't tell whether the exchange is equitable. I don't know the difference between you and me. And I can't live with that.

Ideas do not get concentrated in social interchange; they get spread around. I can patent an object produced from an idea. I can copyright the explanation of an idea. I can get the credit for originating an idea. I can do all those things, but I cannot own an idea. I cannot lose an idea or get rid of it. Even when I stop believing an idea, I still have it stored in my memory as a discredited idea. Even when I hate an idea and make a successful effort to forget it, it shows up in my behavior even after I have forgotten it, and it can crop up in my conscious thought at the most disconcerting times.

It is clear that ideas are different from objects, even though I do talk about them as if they were as concrete as objects. I have never been able to pinpoint the important differences. I am sure, though, that ideas are a basis of power and freedom. I am also sure that ideas cannot be controlled for power the way objects can.

Attempts at censorship are probably as old as communication. As tragically successful as some censorships seem to be, they seem always to have had their limits somewhere in time and space. Perhaps ideas are so important and people search them out from one another because all of us are so fundamentally ignorant. We don't know why we were born; nor do we know why we were born when and where we were. We did not choose our parents and they did not choose us. We do not know how or why we will die or when or where we will die or what will happen after that.

But we need to know. There is so much that we will never know that perhaps, somehow, we need to compensate as much as possible with what we can come to know. And we search for the truth, all of the truth we can come by, all the skills and ideas and feelings we can gather from one another. Ideas can show not only how things are but also how things can be. I think that is why ideas are such hard resources to control as a basis for power.

It is the same with skills. Transfer your skill to others, by whatever methods of training, and you still have the skill, often with new proficiency of your own. With skills and with ideas, interchange does not concentrate them; it spreads them around.

It is even more so with feelings. It is easy to express a feeling and to generate feelings in others. Feelings can be held in, restrained, left unexpressed in any open way, and they become not much good to anyone. They can even become warped and twisted in the restraint and become pretty bad for everybody. Feelings can be expressed and responded to and interchanged right and left. The interchange can give me a lot of trouble if the interchange tells me something I don't want to know, such as how self-centered I am or how I have hurt others or how I have become involved with others. Nobody ever said, though, that my resources would all be happy ones. Resources, all of them—objects, skills, ideas, feelings—like the truth they so imperfectly represent, tell me all sorts of things I don't want to know. If you listen to the way I usually talk and watch the way I usually act, you would think that feelings cause more trouble than anything else, but I'm pretty sure it isn't true. I'm pretty sure that objects, skills, and ideas cause just as much trouble as feelings. It is just that it is easier to deny the kind of trouble an object causes. I can remember the time I put a frog in a little girl's lunch box. Steadfastly I maintained that "it wasn't the thing that caused the trouble; it was her feelings about it." The truth is that it was the feelings that told what the trouble was. What caused the trouble was everything. Just the way it was when I gave my wife that iron skillet for a birthday present. Anyway, the supply of feelings is increased and spread around with human interchange, and through the interchange of feelings, a lot of us can get to know a lot more than we do about our troubles and about our joys—our joys in work, our joys in play, and our joys in love.

On Dependency and Dependability

The interchange of feelings involves specialization, too. Some of us are experts at fighting. We can express criticism well and cope well with destruction, but we must depend upon others to supply the support necessary to rebuild more realistically what we tore apart. Some of us are specialists at support and reassurance, but we find it difficult to fight and we blanch at the fight that is clearly necessary to provide needed criticism. Some of us are specialists in flight. We seem to sense when tension is about to rise past the limits of tolerance, and we can turn a phrase or make a joke or change a subject. Such feelings, such realistic fears, such well-timed flights are needed by others, others who can more skillfully arouse tension in the complacent or support self-esteem in the embarrassed. Some of us are most needed in times of danger, but we are not much good in times of safety. Some of us are most needed in times of poverty, but we are not much good in times of riches. Some of us are most needed in times of challenge, but we are not much good in times of affection. We, all of us, are specialists in the development of emotional resources, and we need each other to supply those emotional resources that we have not developed, and could never quite so well develop, for ourselves.

Several social scientists have proposed that there is a universal norm of reciprocity. It is just possible that all men in all cultures, in some way or another, hold a very deep belief that needed resources received from others ought to be returned, with resources needed by the others. A world full of con men has denied this norm, but at the cost of more dishonor than most of us can stand.

I have been impressed by the power of a simple demonstration used by social scientists. Four or five people are given a ten-dollar bill, with a few simple conditions. They are asked simply to decide which one of them is to get the bill, to be used entirely for his own pleasure. The money cannot be divided, given to a charity, used for a group activity, such as a party, *or repaid in kind to the group*. The recipient cannot be selected by lot. The group must decide by some means to give the bill to one member and one member only.

It is not surprising that the decision is hard to make. Usually each person makes a strong case for giving himself the money. The surprising thing is that it soon becomes apparent, in spite of confusions and denials, that no one really wants the money. No one finds it easy to say why he doesn't want it, but many finally explain, "I haven't done anything for it."

Given pressure from outside and time pressure, the decision usually gets made. The "winner" takes the money reluctantly. He often offers it to the scientist initiating the demonstration, "now that the demonstration is over." But he must keep it and use it for his own pleasure.

Later, days or weeks, the recipient often tries

On Dependency and Dependability

again to return the money or to offer some gift to the group involved. On one occasion, a bright and vigorous young lady approached me a month after the demonstration and said, "Please, please take this money. I can't stand it. I hate it. I can't use it. I can't keep it. Please get me out of this." There really may be a universal norm of reciprocity. There seems to be a very widespread belief that runs deep into the very core of human feelings. You really can't have something for nothing. You pay for it with your peace of mind.

On Dependency and Crises

In an emergency, I can quite voluntarily lie unconscious on a table in surgery while a surgeon literally takes my life in his hands. My dependency is complete. It is not only that I don't understand what he is doing to me, I am unconscious. I don't even know what he is doing. Yet, to me, then and there, my complete dependency is altogether appropriate. I feel no yearning at all for the freedom, or the skill, to perform the surgery myself.

In even a more general emergency, I can become confused and frightened by a sudden unexpected disaster, unaccountably striking down my neighbors and me. In the screaming pain and ugly rubble of a tornado, I have been more than ready to follow any man who was not in panic, who had a loud, clear voice, and who looked as if he knew what he was doing. If he also wore some symbol of authority, that was better. But it was far from necessary. Just let him be in control of himself, purposeful, and loud and clear in his instructions.

The thing that frightens me most about crisis-born dependency is the special danger of exploitation. I have run into all sorts of phony crises trumped up by men who had to find a way to get other people to do what they wanted them to do. Phony time limits are very popular forms of phony crises.

Once, in my time, I was eager to get others to act as I was sure was best for us all, and I was frustrated by the reservations and reluctance of my fellows. In our frustration, it seemed we would argue forever. I warned my fellows that our time was short and I said, "We must stop wasting it!" I knew that we were afraid of failure, and I used the fear of failure to make the time available seem shorter than it really was. Once I had voiced the warning, my fellows were ready and willing to believe that we must act quickly. The mood of the working team changed abruptly. Before my warning, the team was concerned, prudent—and self-reliant. Now it was tense, desperate—and dependent. I could present my views quickly and clearly. My plan was quickly adopted. I remember well how desperately my fellows said, "We have no other alternative!"

Later, when the defects of the plan had become so embarrassingly apparent, it was said, "In view of the time demands on us, it was the best we could do. We had no other alternative!" Over the years, I have grown more and more suspicious of that assertion: "There is nothing else we can do." I have grown more and more suspicious of time limits that are set by those who have the authority and the responsibility for the work, especially when they are concerned about the exercise of their authority and the weight of their responsibility. It has become important to me to understand whether the limits have been set in the interest of wise budgeting of time or whether they have been set in the interest of producing a phony crisis. I know so well how a phony crisis makes it easier for an ambitious man to get others to do what he wants them to do.

I have learned, from many lessons, how crises create tensions in people and how rising tensions cut down the number of resources a fellow can see —the number of alternative ways a fellow can see out of the crisis. Action, any action, is better than the awful pressure of the tension, and men like me take foolish actions. I was once grimly sobered by a dramatic story taken from some studies of the communications among Japanese leaders during the deliberations that led to the decision to bomb Pearl Harbor. As the tensions grew higher, the number of alternatives considered grew fewer. Finally, as the fateful orders were issued, one responsible leader wrote in his diary something like this: "There come times in the lives of nations, as in the lives of men, when there is nothing left but to jump from the roof of the temple."

About Dependency on People and Procedures
Having felt that depending on people produced injustice and exploitation, I have found myself turning to dependency on procedures. Procedures can provide order and clarity when people are disorderly and confusing. Often, for me, the profits of clarity and understanding are worth the costs in dependency, dependency on the procedures instead of on the good sense of my fellows and me.

The trouble with procedures is that they can become more important than the decisions to be made. When they do, I have to look back at the procedures again to try to find out how they got started and what kinds of decision-making they fit best.

In trying to learn about dependency and dependability in organizational decision-making, it seems to me that the first thing to do is to rule out the situation where one man has all the resources necessary to make valid and wise decisions which affect the lives of all the other people in the organization. In such a situation, if it ever really exists, decision-making is rather easy, even if it is pretty degrading for all the people except the one man.

It seems to me that there are some other basic assumptions to be made clear and explicit, too. I think you have to assume that people hold significantly different viewpoints, and their posi-

On Dependency and Dependability

tions on the issues change as the issues change. You have to assume that the decision requires both specialized knowledge and more general judgment in fitting together the special knowledge. Both the validity and the wisdom of the decision require the consideration of a wide range of ideas and opinions, and you have to assume that interpersonal communication is an effective way of making ideas and opinions available for consideration. As well as I can tell, most people take these assumptions for granted, but I think it is important to state them explicitly.

I think there are three kinds of procedures for decision-making which are widely used and widely confused these days. The oldest is the traditional parliamentary procedure. I think parliamentary procedure was developed by men in low political power positions to limit the power of men in higher positions. It makes men dependent on the judgment of the majority of men, and that is probably better than being dependent on the judgment of one man. In business and professional life, where authority and responsibility involve personal ownership of capital or personal attainment of competence—and the personal courage to risk money or reputation—it seems easier to depend upon the rule of personal authority. Executives need and get all sorts of advice, but the one executive or the one professional practitioner in authority makes the critical decisions. In science, sometimes in professional affairs, and occasionally in business

and politics, people lose faith in formal procedures and decisions get made by consensus,
both public and private. Dependency on consensus is the most vague kind of dependency.
It is often more trying and prolonged, but it
gives each person the most freedom to decide
how he will contribute to the decision-making.

It seems to me that each of these three—parliamentary, executive, and consensus—must
have its own time and place. Surely there is a
time for the rule of the majority, a time for the
rule of authority, and a time for the rule of consensus. In the following, I want to try to say what
I have felt and thought about the meaning of
dependency on procedures and of the dependability of procedures.

About Dependency on the Rule of the Majority
I would guess that the most honored, the most
abused, and the most subverted decision-making method is based on the rule of the majority
and parliamentary procedure. There is a story
told about W. C. Fields when he was in the hospital with a terminal cancer. A friend knew that
Fields was aware that he was dying. He came to
visit the old cynic with great apprehension
about how to approach him. On entering the
room, he found Fields propped up in bed, reading the Bible. The friend was quite plainly startled. Fields, always tickled to taunt his friends,
held up the Bible and said, "I'm looking for
loopholes." Decision-making procedures have

always been fair game for subversion among men who distrust power.

Many people forget that parliamentary procedure itself must be agreed upon, and the traditional way to get such an agreement on procedure is to seek a consensus. It is never clear just what is meant by "consensus," but it involves a belief or feeling among a group of people that they have grasped "the sense of the meeting" and that they can proceed with confidence enough that each member has a similar understanding and will do just about what is expected of him.

Once there is consensus on procedure—and it may take some false starts to know whether there is—the traditional assumption of parliamentary procedure is that the decision must be made in the face of conflicting and mutually exclusive interests among the members. A decision in accord with the interests of any one man necessarily will be at odds with the interests of others. The prime assumption is that reconciliation is impossible. One of the great strengths of parliamentary decision-making is that it can produce workable decisions in the face of a firm and continuing conflict of interests. The whole thing came out of the growth of the English Parliament. Whether barons or freemen, these Englishmen had to cope with kings and men who believed the powers of the kings were given to them by an all-knowing God. That sort of thing did not lead to much confidence in the reconciliation of conflicts of interest. The important thing, I think, was that the conflicts of interest took in many men. Parliamentary methods have been useful *within* labor unions, legislatures, boards of directors, and town meetings. They haven't helped much to resolve conflicts *between* one owner and a group of workers, one president and a resistant Congress, or one dictator and an intimidated people.

One of the great evils of parliamentary decision-making is that it has been imposed when there really were mutual interests and there only seemed to be conflicts of interest. Parliamentary decision-making has forced men to take sides and thereby produced a sense of conflicts of interest when, in fact, there was no real conflict. Before I decide whether I want to depend upon a majority rule to deal with a conflict of interests, it is critically important to me to judge whether the conflict is really there. If it isn't, the parliamentary method is probably not the best approach to decision-making.

There is another traditional assumption in the parliamentary approach that seems often overlooked and, to me, seems of great importance. The method was created to deal with, but not to settle, issues about *values*. The underlying question was: "What is good and what is bad?" More often it was more practical and less categorical: "What is better and what is worse?" If each man

On Dependency and Dependability

is entitled to the right to decide for himself what he believes is good and what he believes is bad, a continuing conflict of values is likely. If living together requires that we have some reasonably sound mutual expectations about how we are to act—not believe, just act—it is necessary for us to reach some decisions about what actions we can expect of each other, temporarily, at the very least. The parliamentary method has achieved its greatest glory as a way of making decisions about what *actions* can be expected in the face of irresolvable conflict about what is good and what is bad.

A part of its glory, too, has been the acceptance of the assumption that all such decisions are temporary. If enough people change their views about what is to be done, then the majority hold a new view. The decision is changed, even reversed. Perhaps underlying all of this is the assumption that nobody—individual or group, majority or minority—knows what is good in any permanent way. The decisions are about how to act, not how to believe. As beliefs change in the search for what is good, the decisions and actions must change, too. I'm pretty sure, traditionally, that the focus on issues of value and the insistence on reversible decisions gave a minority group two great resources. The minority still could hold to their beliefs with dignity and even try to convince others of their validity, so long as their actions conformed to the majority decision. The decision would always be reversed if enough people changed their votes about needed actions.

Both my fellows and I have, at times, tried to apply parliamentary methods to decisions which are not matters of values. No landslide of votes can change the fact that the big moon spins round the earth. It can change how much of our energy we use spinning small moons round the earth. So much do facts grow from actions and actions from values that it is hard to tell what is a matter of value and what is a matter of fact.

There are few times when a man is more dependent on others than when he is being tried before a jury. On a jury on which I served, the issue was stated as an issue of guilt, not an issue of fact. The jury was supposed to accept all testimony as fact, all the facts. No votes about facts. The issue was to decide whether the accepted facts left any doubt about the guilt of the defendant. I discovered that for most people, however, the question about the guilt of the defendant was a matter of fact, too, and the distinction was not really a very useful one. I suppose that I would agree that the decision becomes critical, and the method important, when the fact of the guilt was so unclear that the values and beliefs we held began to influence our votes. Perhaps it was just precisely the points where the testimony was inconclusive that the method became critical. The unanimity required in that parliamentary decision-making became the appropriate insurance, because, under those conditions, the jury was deciding on a grave action to be taken in the face of insufficient facts and a deep conflict of values. The action became the important part. Agreement on action had to be separated from agreement on values. It was too hard for me to vote "guilty" under those conditions, and I "hung" the jury.

The confusion leads me to too many distortions of the method and to too many dependencies with which I feel uncomfortable. I have participated in procedures by which parliamentary methods have been used to determine the color of a car, the effect of a chemical, the appropriateness of a surgical operation, the market price of brick, the prevalence of drug addiction, the feelings experienced by a person who was present, and, on one bizarre occasion, whether or not it was raining at Yankee Stadium.

Sometimes the rule of the majority was invoked because we were impatient with the arguments about the validity of the data available, such as the color of a car when the car was no longer available to see. Sometimes it was because it was easier than more objective methods that were readily available to seek the fact, such as the market price of brick. Sometimes it was because we did not trust the people who had access to technical data, such as the effects of sodium fluoride in the drinking water. Sometimes it was because we did not want to know the facts, such as whether it was raining at

Yankee Stadium. The facts would frustrate us. I've often thought that it must be a great problem to the parliaments of the world to make so many decisions about matters of the values to be placed upon the uses and misuses of science these days. It seems important that the highly specialized and technical knowledge available to scientists be made available to parliaments when they must decide, for example, how much of a nation's resources should be allocated to the advancement of knowledge about a particular disease or about a particular exploration of space. Deciding about the value of man's going to the moon must be at once as ridiculous as a nursery rhyme, as technically complicated as astronomy, and as profound as the contemplation of man's need to grasp the meaning of the infinity of space.

The issue is: What is of value? The decision is: What is to be done?

The *dependency* is on the safety of numbers in a majority rule. Action is guided by what most people think, no matter what is ultimately good. The limits on the dependency lie in the limits on how much the issue is a question of value and how much it is a question of fact. On questions of fact, dependency on the rule of the majority is silly. In a conflict of value, dependency on the rule of the majority to get agreement on an action may be one of man's best hopes.

The *dependability* is in the confidence one can

On Dependency and Dependability

have in expecting others to behave in accord with the majority rule, no matter what they believe. The limits on the dependability lie in the limits on how long the decision will last, how long before the majority changes its views.

There is another assumption upon which we depend, often unrealistically, in parliamentary decision-making. We assume that public debate assures the authenticity of the viewpoints expressed. It does seem reasonable that, given an opportunity to speak his mind and the responsibility to do it in public and be heard by all, each man will say what he really believes. It seems to be reasonable, but I have often found that I could not depend upon it. Parliamentary or not, I have found myself, in decision-making endeavors, feeling the old urge to influence the decision. Not satisfied to express my view clearly and cast my vote humbly, I wanted to influence the way others expressed their views and cast their votes, even to influence the votes of many, so that the decision would go my way. Once I think about it, it seems incredible that I would say something I didn't really believe or that I would try to induce others to say something they really didn't believe, but that is the way it has been. So long as bargaining or belonging, instead of believing, influence the expression of views and the casting of votes, a fellow cannot depend upon the assumption that public debate assures a genuine public expression of one's beliefs.

As I look back, I think that parliamentary decision-making has too long and too honorable a history to be discarded. It may be our best bet for controlling conflicts of values which can't be resolved, at least as long as we cherish the belief that each man is entitled to his own personal views about what is good. It has been responsible for some of the world's most important victories over tyranny. It has also been tragically corrupted and unthinkingly subverted by all sorts of bargaining for power and all sorts of angling for membership in special groups. When can I depend upon it? How can I depend upon it? When can I be a dependable part of it? How can I be a dependable part of it?

How shall I know that the issue is a conflict of values and not a determination of facts? How shall I discover whether the method is creating a conflict of views that did not exist before it was invoked? How shall a voter gain access to any specialized knowledge, the value of which he must judge? How shall I help ensure that public debate stimulates genuine expression of viewpoints and not deceitful efforts to win debates? How shall I base my vote on what I believe, how shall I resist what I'd like to bargain for, and how shall I resist the prestige and power of groups to which I'd like to belong?

These are the questions I must keep trying to answer if I am to learn more about when to depend upon the rule of the majority to provide a dependable way of controlling conflicts of beliefs about what is good. That is where I am in thinking about parliamentary decision-making.

About Dependency on the Rule of Authority
It seems to me that it is important to distinguish another kind of decision-making which is more often invoked when personal authority and responsibility are involved. The authority can be based upon position, competence, or popularity, but, however based, it is authority delegated to one man. It is seldom concerned with issues of values. Seldom, outside the church, is one man delegated the authority and given responsibility (although many have tried to take it) to decide for others about what is good. It is often concerned with issues of technology, of professional practice, of strategy and tactics, of marketing and financing—in short, questions of how to reach a goal rather than what a goal should be.

Such executive decision-making is authoritative but not, I think, authoritarian. Many people influence the decision. It is just that only one man is responsible for it. An executive can take one key assumption seriously. He can really believe that no one man can have all the resources needed to make important decisions without assistance. If you watch such executives at work, you can see them try hard to surround themselves with competent advisors. They seek staff men and line men who are competent enough, and confident enough, to inform them clearly and advise them honestly.

Another key assumption is hard to take seriously. It is hard to assume very firmly that the staff tell the boss what they really think, not just what they think he wants to hear. You remember the tag line: "I want you gentlemen to tell me exactly what you think, even if it costs you your job."

When I have been asked to advise the boss, I have gotten into a lot of trouble by telling the boss just exactly what I believed. I have also gotten into a lot of trouble by not telling him just exactly what I believed. At times it has seemed to be a game I couldn't win. I got into trouble and the boss got into trouble and others got into trouble, because it wasn't really a game, it was serious business. Our mistakes misguided people and deprived people and hurt people. It wasn't a game at all.

You can find a lot of gamesmanship in this informing and advising in executive decision-making. Looking back on my troubles with it, I remember a time when I had to advise an aggressive boss who very badly wanted to hire a man he liked to have around, a man he knew to have repeatedly shown poor judgment in his work. I think I felt that if I could convince myself that it was all just a game, I could in turn convince myself that it would be foolish to take the game too seriously. I would be foolish to risk an important career, my career, on the weakening self-control of a man who was already on the spot because he must make a difficult and risky decision. It would surely be foolish to make him mad at me. Justified or not, his opinions of me really would have important effects upon my career. To be dependable meant to start a fight. Surely it was not the time to fight. Surely it was a time to run away.

I told him what I thought he wanted to hear; I told him to hire the man. I told myself it was all a game anyway. The thing to do was to play the game and take only small risks and not toss away a career on a game.

I can't be sure, but I think that is the way it often goes when a man is called upon to advise a boss and a boss is called upon to take all the responsibility for a difficult and risky decision. An executive can be painfully lonely and vulnerable and dependent. There is no way, no way at all, by which he really can be sure that his staff members are dependable, that they are telling him what they really think or just what they think he wants to hear.

Even when the decision-making goes well and the advice comes competently and clearly and honestly, the boss must sweat. No matter how much he has depended upon the information and advice of his staff, the decision is his, not theirs. When the decision goes into action and works well or poorly, he is responsible. It is this lonely vulnerability that has made it hard for me, when I have been on the spot, to be as careful as I might to be sure I will have valid data on which to judge whether the thing is working in action.

Judging when to stop the action and start the thinking again has been hard for me, too. It is easy to say that it is important to allow any plan to be tried long enough to give a basis to judge how well it is working. It is easy to say, also, that you must not allow it to go so long that you can't back up and correct its mistakes. It is easy to say, but it is hard to do.

You really are on the spot. No matter how much you are paid for it, you really are on the spot. I have listened with close attention, evaluated with real concern, and organized with careful effort all that my staff has had to say. I have exercised my authority and made my decision on my own, knowing full well that, as critical as the staff work was, I alone must take the consequences of the decision. If it worked well, the reward would be mine. If it worked poorly, the humiliation would be mine. To work hard to provide for a hardheaded kind of feedback from the decision in action could be working hard to humiliate yourself. It is taking a big risk, a frightening risk, and it isn't easy to do it. It is much easier to get the feedback through indirect channels, from friendly people, and in the form of opinions that necessarily have to be vague, subjective, and susceptible to bias.

It is a very widespread idea that, in modern social organizations, it is absolutely essential that authority be accompanied by responsibility, and that both be allocated so that for every decision there is one, and only one, person with the authority and responsibility. I have come to think that this is an obsolescent idea.

Is the idea of individual responsibility consistent with the idea that no one man can have all the resources needed to make important decisions? It is not consistent with the practice of executive decision-making through the confusing and distorted route of advice-giving. Actually, many men contribute in one way or another to the making of the decision. It is not consistent with the practice of distributing rewards. The one man with sole authority is not actually allowed to make the sole determination of how the organizational rewards, usually pay and prestige, are to be distributed, either between him and his subordinates or even among his subordinates.

The idea of individual responsibility may have some basis in the idea that, when things go wrong, it is necessary to know whom to punish. There is a widespread idea that almost nobody will accept the blame for a failure, that almost everybody puts the blame on somebody else. I would like to suggest that it is very unlikely that the cause of a failure can be found in one person. In the complex social organizations in which we live, failure must have multiple causes involving many people. The loss of resources to the organization which can follow from mistakes is almost automatically allocated to many of the members, never quite justly, to be sure, never quite equitably, for justice and equity are ideals. However explicit or implicit, however just or equitable, some sort of agreement about reciprocity is very probably a necessary condition for any sort of regular function in a social organization. To intervene in this reciprocal allocation of resources by insisting that the loss must be taken by only one man is not only arbitrary and punitive, it is also unrealistic and impossible to accomplish. It may well be more practical to intervene to modify the allocation in the interest of justice and equity. It is, at least, not so arbitrary to try to see that each member of the organization receives that share of the loss most nearly proportional to his contribution to the mistake. The goals of justice and equity are idealistic; they are never reached. I prefer idealism to punitiveness. Justice and equity can be approached, and the approach can be less and less arbitrary as we learn.

There is also a very old and cherished idea that no man can serve two masters. Maybe it could have come from the belief that no man can serve two gods. God is all-knowing and all-powerful. Man knows hardly anything and has very little influence on the scheme of things. The idea may have fit the affairs of men when some men were supposed to have had divine origins or divine rights, but I propose here, as soberly as I can, that the idea doesn't fit now. Each of us must satisfy all sorts of people with almost everything we do. We must satisfy our

On Dependency and Dependability

superiors, we must satisfy our friends, we must satisfy our subordinates, we must satisfy our families, we must satisfy our police authorities, we must satisfy our health authorities, we must satisfy our church authorities, we must satisfy even our memories of all those significant people whose judgment we have respected in our time. Each of them has contributed some resources to our lives and stimulated some promises for our lives, and we must, according to our idea of an equitable interchange, contribute at least some degree of respect and some promise-keeping in return.

In the office of one experienced, perceptive, and courageous state health officer, I learned something of what it means to be clearly dependable in the exercise of authority and to be equally clearly dependent on the work of a subordinate. I also learned how dependency and dependability and fight and flight are all bound up with human support. He was reviewing his work and his problems with his advisors They knew him well, they were competent men, and they wanted to advise him well.

He was in a reflective mood. "We have tried too many new things. That means taking risks—risks with human lives. It's not that we shouldn't take risks. A lot is at stake. I have a duty to take calculated risks on careful ideas. I don't even mind gambling on my own competence—risking my reputation. I'm not fainthearted that way. . . ."

He trailed off, and after a moment one of his

staff said, "A man can't be fainthearted and build a working health department out of a pork barrel the way you did. And did you ever. . . ."

"I know," he interrupted. "I've shouted down a lot of tough guys, but . . ." He stopped again pensively, but it was clear that he was going to say more.

"I don't like it. Fighting with tough guys makes me cringe inside while I trick them or trap them or beat them down. It makes me uncomfortable. Very uncomfortable."

"Nobody likes conflict."

"Makes everybody uncomfortable."

"No," he said quietly. "Some men thrive on it. They really love a good fight. You, Floyd," he continued, turning to his senior staff member. "You are excited by a fight. You use your power and your brain well and hard. You're challenged by the chance to win a contest, to control an argument."

"I'm not sure it's a virtue," said Floyd, "but it's true of me."

"The world of public policy is full of men like you, and they're needed. They meet issues head on. They're specialists in aggression. They're fight managers, fight specialists. They get important work done. But, by nature, I'm not one of them."

All of us knew this was important to him, but we just weren't sure what was tearing at him. I turned to him. "We're not really with you, Chuck. What are you getting at?"

On Dependency and Dependability

"I want to appoint a man to be my fight specialist."

"Why, Chuck?"

"I like the way *you* fight." This came from Floyd.

"I don't." Chuck spoke quietly. "I'm very good at planning, at new program development, at long-range finance, at calculating risks. But I'm not good at fighting."

"You're good enough with me."

"The fact is that I don't like to confront conflict. Oh, I do it. I don't like to surrender either. But my first impulse is to back away—too quickly, too much."

"Are you telling us you're too skittish for your job?" The question was a sharp one and Chuck flinched a little.

"Maybe," he said. "I want the use of a better fighter than I am, but I want him to fight for what I want, I guess, or what we can agree all of us want to fight for."

"You're asking for a hired gun." The statement was civil enough, but there was a clear tone of contempt in it. Chuck was hurt, but he was challenged, too.

"You could say that all right. But you could say that I am able to recognize what I do well and what I do poorly. You could say that I want to capitalize on what I do well, on the really significant contributions I can make...." Chuck spoke steadily until that point and then he seemed to be involved in his thoughts.

"Yeah," he said suddenly, as if he were speaking to himself. "Sometimes when I avoid a conflict on the spot, I go home and I can't stop thinking about it. I toss and turn at night and I wake up and suddenly I snap to and say, 'Sure! That's what I should have done. That would have met it head on and settled it then and there.' And I wish I wouldn't be so damned inhibited; I wish I would barrel into the fray then and there and I am ashamed of myself." Chuck stopped and looked directly at us, excited and searching.

"But I shouldn't be. I am in a trap. If I fight, I am strained and unnatural. If I don't, I am ashamed of myself. That's why I say we need some division of labor. We need a man who is naturally challenged by a conflict, who likes to fight a good, clean fight. He could take a big load off me. I can concentrate on what I do best and leave the fighting to a specialist."

Chuck stopped. He seemed to be clear in his position now. The staff were concerned and worried. I needed to make one thing clear.

"Are you asking Floyd to be the fight specialist?"

"I would like him to think about it, yes."

"Floyd?"

"I'm willing to think about it. I guess I'm good at fights."

The staff were quiet. Each man looked anxiously at the others. Finally someone said, "The decision is yours, Chuck, even if you are afraid to make it. In the end, it's your neck."

"That's right," said Chuck, "that's the way it is."

After the meeting, Chuck was depressed. When we two were in his office again, he said, in a quiet and thoughtful tone, "The thing is right, you know. Emotional specialization is as important as any other kind of specialization." He stopped, and then, "But in the world I live in, I'm going to look like a coward." He paused again reflectively, and then, "I'll never really know what my own staff think. And I need their support, because I am very vulnerable. Alone, I may never know for sure whether I really am a coward."

If one could abandon the idea that only one person must be responsible for organizational decisions, it might be possible to put more honesty and realism into executive decision-making. The lonely vulnerability of the executive could be reduced quite a lot. It seems to me that the relief might free him from trying to be something he can never be, whether he tries to be the unflinchingly rough and tough competitor, the unrealistically wise and knowing mentor, or the unbelievably slick and cynical sophisticate. The dependency of his subordinates on his objectivity could be considerably relieved, and the relief might free them to express their ideas and feelings more openly. The executive's search for hard data on *the*, not *his*, decisions in action could be significantly extended, and they might free the whole system to depend upon concrete data rather than upon abstract authority for the resources they need in the search for organizational competence.

About Dependency on Consensus

For some time now, there has been all around me a continuing concern about developing a new approach to social decision-making. Wouldn't it be simpler, clearer, and better all around if all those who will be affected by the decision regularly participate in, and equitably influence, the making of the decision? My experiences with the various approaches to participative decision-making have led to some confusing results. Sometimes the decisions just don't get made, even when there is plenty of time for making them. Sometimes they get made, but they aren't very satisfactory to anyone. Most often, if the decision-making goes well, there is more than satisfaction with the decision. It is a real pleasure to see how much more commitment there is to such decisions and how much more readily and competently the decision is implemented, if it goes well. This sort of thing, as is abundantly clear by now, leads me to ask questions.

What are the assumptions which underlie participative decision-making? Is it assumed that the individuals involved can reach some genuine agreement about what is good and bad or what is better or worse—agreement on values? Or is it like other decision-making, confining itself to decisions about some concrete action to be taken, not requiring the participants to take a single position about values in the abstract? It must be so, because, if each human is to be free to satisfy his own conscience about what is good and what is bad, surely one cannot aspire to agreement on what is good in the abstract. Or can it be that consensus requires some agreement upon values among the participants in order to produce a commitment to act in accord with the decision?

Is it assumed that each member has equal influence upon the decision? Can it be that each participant's influence upon the decision will vary with the respect of the group for his knowledge, ideas, and opinions about the matters in question, whether specialized or general? Is it possible that the judgment of the participants about the true competence of one of their number can be realistic?

Is it possible for a group to determine, as a part of its decision-making, just what evidence will be acceptable as evidence of the success or failure of the implemented decision? Is it possible to reach a consensus about the acceptability of evidence when all the evidence obtainable is subjective or ambiguous?

How does a group make use of resources, such as knowledge, skill, and familiarity, which are not to be found within the group? Must a consultant become a participant? If influence upon the decision is to be determined by the respect of the group for knowledge, opinions, and ideas of the participant, how can the influence of a consultant be determined in some other way?

As I have raised these questions, some propositions have come to mind. As well as I can interpret my experiences with participative decision-making, it seems to me that all of the following propositions are involved in it: The participants have complementary values and interests, not conflicting ones. Differing but complementary values and interests can be satisfied by the same decision. The influence of each participant will vary from time to time and question to question in accord with the respect of the group for his ideas and opinions. Specialized resources from outside the group can be provided by consultants, whose influence will be in accord with the respect of the group for their ideas and opinions. The authenticity of the expressed viewpoints of the participants will vary with the capacity of the group to tolerate disagreement and the hostility which accompanies it. The decision can be made by consensus without any explicit general agreement about just what "consensus" is. The group will believe a consensus has been reached when, in fact, many participants do not agree with, and are not committed to implement, the decision. A part of the decision-making process is the testing of an apparent consensus against the commitment of the participants to implement the decision.

The decision is considered to be an experimental action and includes a commitment to the acceptance of imperfect data as adequate evidence of the outcome of the experiment. Such experimental actions are provisional and short-term, always subject to reconsideration and modification as the data come in. The decision-making process is a kind of circle of thinking and deciding and acting and evaluating and thinking and deciding and acting and evaluating and around and around, all the time in the hope that we are learning more about what life is like. Such participative decision-making still has the wonderful advantage of the dependability of the implementation, an advantage that parliamentary and executive decision-making often do not supply. It is my guess that it isn't very satisfactory for managing the tensions involved in mutually contradictory views about what is good and what is bad. The parliamentary method, with all its susceptibility to subversion, may still be the best hope for coping with such value conflicts. It is also my guess that it is not much good for making decisions for which one person is authorized and responsible. I would gamble even on the lonely vulnerability of the executive with his advisors. But, if the issue is one of learning from experience, where experimental, provisional attempts to solve problems are possible; if the authority and responsibility can be shared according to some tentatively acceptable norm of reciprocity; and if one can solve the very difficult problem of meeting the assumptions about the tolerance of emotional expression, the capacity for authenticity, the patience with false consensus, and the availability of acceptable data—if these obtain, I would prefer to gamble on participative decision-making. And I would remember how much all social decision-making is a gamble. I would remember that what I am gambling on is my judgment and that of my fellows about when to be dependent and when to be dependable and how to be dependent and how to be dependable.

On the Quest for Justice

As long as I live with other people, I find myself dependent and I find myself dependable, whether I mean to be or not. There are some resources I must develop for myself, partly because I need them to be available unconditionally, anywhere, anytime (such as stamina), and partly because I need them for my self-respect (such as courage). Some resources I must depend upon others to supply for me, partly because I could not supply them so well for myself (such as surgical skill), and partly because I like others to do some things for me (such as making great music). That is the way I find myself dependent, but my feelings about reciprocity run deep in me. I cannot live very long in debt and still be at peace with myself.

On Dependency and Dependability

Some resources I can supply to others more readily than they can supply them for themselves, and I find I must supply them, partly because I want to produce a fair return for what I receive, and partly because I like to do some things for other people.

Each day I change and the world changes. My ideas about what is fair change. How many resources do I want to have available? At what price? Does freedom mean having available the resources I need when and where I need them? At what price? My needs change and my ideas about what I need change. Does freedom mean knowing what I really need without fooling myself? Or is freedom an illusion?

Is it power I am after? Do I want resources available so that others can influence me no more than I believe is fair? Do I want resources available so that I can influence others—no more than they believe is fair? How much power do I want to have? How much power ought I to have?

How well aware am I of the changes in the world which stimulate its people to seek new resources, new freedom, and new power? How well can I see the new attempts to control motives, feelings, and ideas: the motives, feelings, and ideas of the engineer with his powerful buttons to push; of the surgeon with his godlike scalpel; of the producer with his television camera; of the priest with his hotline to guilt; of the judge with his command of legalized force;

and of the man in the street with his contagious emotions and the voice of the crowd?

All this is to ask again when to be dependent and when to be dependable, how to be dependent and how to be dependable? These questions are at the very core of the never-ending human quest for justice.

4

On Love—Sought and Offered

On When to Offer Love and How to Offer Love

Love is so simple and so complicated. The power and tenderness of love excite me and puzzle me and annoy me, and I say it is a crazy world that such depth of human support is so sorely needed and so often lost.

To offer love in any simple, honest, and straightforward way is painfully awkward for me, and, except in a special atmosphere, it is embarrassing to others. To ask for love in any simple, honest, and straightforward way is almost impossible for me, and, without careful preparation, startling to others. Just to accept a frank and open offer of love in any simple, natural way is usually incredibly confused and awkward for me.

Love is often expressed at special times and private places, but, for me, everyday life is full of all sorts of love in all sorts of forms—mostly vague—almost as if we wanted to be sure that the love could be denied in case any trouble arose. Sometimes a quick surge of felt affection can override most other feelings, but a lasting love broadens and deepens other feelings. In a lasting love, fights are more intense, flights are more desperate, dependency is more abject, dependability more vital. I think the intense effects of love on fight and flight and dependency make part of the awkwardness in expression, but there is more to it than that.

Time and again, when I feel deeply affectionate, or feel the deep affection of another, I find myself all wound up in myself, in a way strangely foreign to the simple, deep warmth I feel. In this wound-up state, I say all sorts of things to myself.

Love, I say, is simple—not complicated, free—not awkward, and joyful—not painful. But I find that love is complicated and awkward and painful for two people who have been hurt by exposing their love.

Love, I say, is a feeling not a thought. But I find that love is thought, too. I have spent an incredible amount of time thinking about love, and I have almost lost my love when it was thoughtless.

Love, I say, is an experience not a construction But I find that love can be constructed. Some of the greatest loves I have known grew from clearly contrived constructions.

Love, I say, is an offer not a demand. But I find that to express love is to make a demand. If I say, "I love you," unless you are a cynic, you feel a great demand to say, "I love you, too," even if you don't. It is a humane response even if it is a foolish one.

Love, I say, is an intimacy not an exhibition. But I find that love must even be public on occasions. Marriages are public exhibitions of the vows of love.

Love, I say, is a pride not a shame. But I find that love can be shameful. For most humans it may have to be shameful sometimes, because it is so easy to exploit a lover.

Love, I say, is a strength in itself not a weakness.

But I find that, to be freely expressed, love must be open to exploitation. That's why love can be a weakness too.

Love, I say, is a warmth not a lust. But I find that love is partly lust, too. It's a very fuzzy border, the border between fulfillment and gratification.

Love, I say, is human support not a commodity. But I find that the expression of love takes myriad forms, in objects, gestures, skills, and those things are exchanged. Surely there must be both giving and receiving in the living of love.

As a boy with fuzz on my chin, I grew to love a bright and pretty and zestful girl in my school. In time I found myself confronted with my girl— in secure privacy, in warm mood, and in an expectant air. I struggled to express my love and I found my pulse racing, my brow cold and wet, and my mouth as dry as dry. In the midst of what I knew to be a real deep feeling of great affection, I was scared stiff. Again and again I tried to form the tender words that raced through my mind, until, in the end I forced myself to choke out my words of love in clumsy blurts. My stumbling words were nothing like my warm and tender and loving feelings.

Once it was over, once I had said it, and she'd kissed me, the whole of life was free and joyful. That was the way it was, and, in different ways and different forms, that is the way it has always been for me.

As it turned out, time and life separated us from

each other. We longed for each other for some time, grieved deeply over our loss, and grew away from each other. Our love was no less love because we grew away from it, and for me it was a critical point in life when I lived in full and learned in full the strange and touching awkwardness of offering a true and deeply felt love.

In the cool air of any early morn, I can see that offering love makes me feel awfully exposed. Clearly, love is very personal and intimate and I don't want to be personal and intimate just anywhere. But that's not really the exposure that frightens me. I feel very vulnerable, vulnerable to being hurt. In my time, I have offered love and found myself a fool, exploited and ridiculed by a cruel cynic or just righteously attacked by an unsuspecting maiden who deeply resented my embarrassing her. From whatever source it came, it hurt, and it hurt deeply. My love is me, the very most personal, private, intimate me. To reject my love is to reject me in the most painful way. Must it be so?

I have known special times when I could offer love to special people as freely, as openly, as joyfully, as confidently, as could be, without one whit of concern about rejection. It was a great feeling I felt, all outgoing. The joy was in the expression itself. All sorts of responses came back in return, and all were fully encountered without pain. Even the most caustic cynic could be clearly heard without the loss of a bit of the joy. No expectations of others were involved, no debts were to be made or paid, no equity was sought, no demands were there for any but the most naturally felt returns. It was easy for others to respond to. It was a very rare and very great event.

At times looking back on those times of open zestful love, warm tears welled up in my eyes, and I thought that real and true love must surely be like those fleeting wisps of joy, totally free, freely offered, freely given, without concern for response. In a way, it sounds right. Surely love can't be bargained for. You either feel it or you don't. But love is not just a fleeting wisp of joy. Love is to be lived, and living love involves more time than that.

Over the years I have known many people trying hard to express warm and tender feelings. I have seen men and women at work devise all sorts of clever incentive plans to offer material rewards for effort and involvement in the work. They would very rarely say that the incentives were expressions of their warm feelings of gratitude and affection to their fellows who shared their involvement in the work. But, I think, it was their way, a most poorly understood and often defeated way, of expressing both gratitude and affection toward their fellows who shared their involvement in the work. A simple, straightforward expression of gratitude and affection would have been seen as an unfair attempt to control—to gain power—based on sentiment rather than on competence. It is fair, it seems, to

allow others to hold power by their competence
to guide the work but unfair to allow others to
hold power based upon mutual affection for involvement in the work. It is fair, it seems, to accept stock options for work accomplishment,
but it is unfair to accept affection options for
work accomplishment.

For women it is especially hard. Once I was
much concerned because an attractive woman
colleague whose husband was out of town
found suddenly that she must enter a hospital
alone, under a frightening threat of a possible
serious illness. I expressed my concern and
offered to take her to the hospital, to stay with
her until she was settled and under good nurs-
ing care. I said, "I'm too fond of you to let you
go alone." She was both pleased and embarrassed, and I said, "I thought you knew I was
fond of you." Her eyes turned toward the floor,
and she said, "I had hoped you liked me for my
work." Then I knew how hard it must be for an
attractive woman to accept warm feelings from
men with whom she works. I knew how hard
it must have been for my friend to be sure her
men colleagues respected her competence at
work and were not just attracted to her appeal
as a woman. Surely I both respected her competence and delighted in her attractiveness.
How was she to know which was which?

I have seen adolescents so tangled up in their
affections and vulnerabilities that they just sat
down and cried. I have seen grown men and

women of long and happy marriages jockey around on the long distance telephone, each trying to get the other to say "I love you" first. I have seen good friends among vigorous men punch and shove each other about to avoid any appearance of weakness or femininity in their feelings for each other. Very few of us object to being loved, but to accept love with simple trust requires a special sensitivity, a special strength, and a special courage. At some terrible times, when I have felt deeply affectionate or have felt the deep affection of another, I have found myself all wound up in myself, in a way strangely foreign to the simple deep warmth I felt. And I remember an evening a long time ago.

I was visiting an old friend, the resident head of a girls' dormitory in a traditional women's college. It was a cold winter's night. We had been sitting before the fire in big, high-backed chairs at one end of one of those large, lobby-like living rooms so typical of girls' dormitories. My friend had left to attend to some duty or other in her office. As I sat waiting I heard the voices of two youngsters approaching, then stopping. I became aware that they had taken seats on a couch, back to back with me. They didn't know I was behind them. Their voices had a familiar quality. The casual way in which they tossed off their comments wasn't quite consistent with the pitch of their voices. I smiled wisely at first, but then I recognized myself. When I was at college age, it was acutely important to me to be sophisticated, to be hardened against the wounds I had suffered when naïvely I had exposed my needs to young extortionists. The young need affection most acutely and exploit affection most cynically. I remembered how it was for me. Simply to offer open love was too naïve. What I didn't understand then was that it was too dangerous. I might get hurt. My reverie was interrupted as the couple started their conversation again. I was too closely identified not to eavesdrop.

"You look tired," she was saying.

"Yeah. Been drinking a lot. Can't seem to break the cycle. Bunch of fellows go out on the prowl every night, you know, liquor and girls, all part of it." He had that familiar note again, that phony defensive callousness.

"You do look thinner," she maintained the mood.

"Can't seem to eat right."

"Yeah." She added in a bored tone. They were quiet for a time until he turned the conversation toward her.

"Guess college is OK, huh?"

"It's a bore."

"For you?"

"I have these spells," she said in the same tone of the hardened victim of fate.

"Spells?" He showed a little surprise.

"I get wild."

"How you mean, wild?"

"Wild, I scream."

"You mean here, at school?" He was clearly surprised. She had him now.

"Everybody worries about me."

"Wild spells. That's new for you."

"Yeah, no more sweet little Betty."

"Yeah, Betty, the psycho!" He was willing to be impressed, and he moved quickly into her mood of ill-starred destiny. He said sadly,

"We're a mess."

"Aren't we?"

For a long time they said nothing. I could feel two real people under all that exchange of sad destiny, straining every fiber of their being to offer love, and in every straining act they were holding each other at bay.

"Your note," he began again. "You wanted to see me."

"I did. I did. I said I did." She was upset now.

"I wasn't really sure."

"I was clear enough. What do you want for an invitation?"

"It was a long time before your note. You didn't write. Months."

"Damn you!" It was a whisper but she conveyed all the force of a shout in it. "I want to see you. I said it. I said it. Twice I wrote for you."

"Oh, I . . . It's clear. I just wasn't sure you wanted to see me the way I am now." His voice carried his pain. "No, no . . . ." he began again, and stopped.

"I wanted to see you, sure, I . . ." He could not continue.

She sighed. "We are—we are a mess—a stinking mess."

"Your spells, are they bad for you—I mean your
feelings?"

"I scream."

"Often?"

"Often."

"I see."

They stopped again. It was as if they had come
quite close to what each wanted to say, too
close, and they were running away again.

"You have to study much?"

"I don't study."

"You used to."

"How can I study?"

I heard him move. He had moved toward her
on the couch.

"You seem sad," he said very quietly.

"You do, too."

"Yeah, I'm not the man you once knew."

"You're thinner."

"Yeah, it's rough on me."

"What is?"

"Drinking, not sleeping, running . . ."

He trailed off into silence. No one moved a
muscle.

"You really are sad," she whispered.

"Yeah."

"Both of us are."

"Yeah."

There followed one of the longest periods of
silence I think I ever lived through. They sat

perfectly still. I sat perfectly still. Finally, he broke the silence.

"When do I have to leave the dorm?"

"It closes at ten."

"Soon, huh?"

"Yeah, I guess so." I could barely hear her. The struggle had ended. I came within an inch of walking round my chair and just putting her in his arms. But I was caught by the same powerful emotional force that was keeping them apart. Fear. Fear and embarrassment. I knew it well. I could not break out of it.

They rose. She stood quite still.

"Good night, Betty," he said.

"Good night, Mark," she whispered. He left her standing there. She stood still by the couch for a long time and, finally, walked away.

After a time my friend returned. "I saw Betty and her friend saying goodbye and I waited a bit."

"Is Betty ill in any way? I heard her say she had spells."

"Betty? No." She answered. "Betty is a brilliant student, charming girl, but lately she has been rather sad."

I, too, left the dormitory soon. As I walked out the gate to the street, I was struck by the appearance of a young man sitting on a bench at the bus stop. I stopped in the shadows, and I heard racking sobs just breaking through the fierce manly restraints. It may have been the most painful crying I have ever heard.

On Love—Sought and Offered

By now I have lived a long time with people I love deeply and dearly, people who love me deeply and dearly. By now I have known some magnificent moments of feeling and expressing a free and open love just for the joy of the expression—and love has been simple uncomplicated joy. But rarely. Very, very rarely.

On Love and Being Helpful

In the groups I have studied, the acts more sorely missed by the members were supportive acts, expressing interest, attraction, respect, approval. Leaders most often complain that members don't work or that they withdraw after just one effort to participate. Even a brief look at the activities of the group shows that neither the leader nor the member has made even a small move to offer any support for the one effort. Leaders will study for hours to find provocative questions or issues or incentives to stimulate participation. I am pretty confident that a single supportive act can stimulate more work than a battery of provocative questions, hot issues, or attractive incentives.

In trying to listen to groups in search of support for their participants, I often get the impression that supportive acts are as awkward as offers of love, because perhaps they are a way of expressing one kind of love. Our preoccupation about astute bargaining and about not being taken in by confidence men may have impaired our ability to offer or accept genuine support when it is felt. To support may mean to make our resources too readily available, to make our positive feelings vulnerable to exploitation. If all bargaining must be a fight for advantage, our bargaining constrains human resources, including authentic supportive feelings. How can I offer my support without exposure to exploitation? Very probably, never.

Once having offered love, I can never take it back. If I have exposed myself to unfair demands or if I have made unfair demands on others for the return of love they can't express, I have strained a relationship and I can never return to the old one. But I can maintain the encounter. I can try new ways and times of expressing my positive feelings and watch for your response and the cues it gives us for building a new relationship, not too close, not too distant, for the interchange of the support we both feel and can express.

Once in 1960 a group of my fellows and I were engaged in work in a temporary laboratory in which we were trying to train ourselves and others to be more genuinely and humanly supportive to one another. It was not easy work, but we felt it was important. We were making a little progress, and we decided to take a weekend off.

One of us was a remarkable young lady. She was young and competent and bright and attractive and single. It is a rare combination, and she was a rare person. All of us had come to share the kind of friendship that comes from having worked hard at a trying task. In the spirit of friendship, she told us of her plans for the weekend off. She was going into nearby Washington to meet a friend for dinner and the theater. He was, she said, a man of whom she was very fond and he was quite an eligible bachelor. He was one of those surprised millionaires who found themselves unexpectedly rich on their electronic inventiveness and the electronic adventures in space. He was, she said, also attractive, personable, and vigorous, and she was thinking very seriously about marrying him. Her fellow staff members were happily married, but the men were just a little jealous and the women just a little envious as she left for the weekend.

All of us returned from our recreation on Sunday evening for dinner together. All of us made various kinds of talk and all of us were marking time until Claudia told us about her weekend. In good time, she did.

It was Saturday at dinner, she said, that he had been upset and sad. He and his two partners in the electronic firm had been having a fight. One of the partners had been kicking up all kinds of trouble. It seemed that, from the friend's point of view, the one partner had become so obstinate and obstructionistic that the tension was unbearable. They had decided to dissolve the partnership. "There is," he said, "no alternative."

Claudia thought, "I'm supposed to be learning new things and developing new skills in being supportive and helpful to people. If help is love made useful, perhaps I can be helpful to him.

I'm going to try." So it was that she asked him to tell her more about the problem, to explain to her the when, and where, and how, and who of the conflict.

It was all he needed. He explained at length. Claudia asked at times for clarification, at times for elaboration, at times for explanation, at times for information, consciously avoiding offering opinions or suggestions. And, Claudia thought, it went very well. He was seeing new angles, remembering facts he had forgotten before, checking his biases. All through dinner, during intermission at the theater, while snacking after the show, at brunch on Sunday, and in the park on Sunday afternoon, his views were widening, new ideas were developing, and new feelings were emerging.

It was on that Sunday afternoon in the park that he mentioned, "It's been one of the best weekends of my life. It's been a long time since I've thought through a problem so thoroughly. And, say, I do appreciate your being such a good listener while I talked so much and thought out loud so much."

Claudia was pleased, and in her joy she asked, "How did it happen?"

"Well, it just shows you how important it is to take the time to think about these things. I use time at work to think about electronic problems, but I don't use any time at all to think about problems between people. This weekend I did.

I just took the time to think. Time to think, that's how it happened."

Claudia was beginning to be less pleased. "You think," she asked "that did it, huh? Time to think."

"Yep, that was it. I'll know better now just how important it is to take the time to think." He really meant what he was saying.

By now Claudia wasn't pleased at all. "I was thinking *I* might have had something to do with it," she said, as quietly as she could.

"Oh, you did! You did. I know how hard it is to be a good listener, and you were a very, very good one. I am really deeply grateful." And he was.

Claudia looked around at us and stopped telling the story for a minute. Then, she said, "I think I did a pretty good job of helping him with his problem. I am struck by what can be accomplished when it doesn't matter who gets the credit. But I'm not sure that I am really proud of my work. I do like him and I do know now how close we can be."

"Are you going to marry him?"

Claudia smiled slowly and wistfully and said, "No. No, the man I marry must know the difference between what I do and what he does. That's how he will know the difference between him and me."

Claudia's wistful wisdom made crystal clear the insight I had been seeking. I knew before then that love was giving and receiving, and I knew that people in love sometimes found themselves so close that they often couldn't tell who was feeling what, offering what, getting what. To accept the love of my wife, a real living unique person, must be to know quite sensitively and precisely what she gives and what I take. In our exchange of our love and ideas and motives and feelings and skills, all the resources get transformed into new forms of human life. I am a little different each day, and my wife is a little different each day, partly because of what we interchange and transform in our interaction. But as I grow in the art of accepting her love, I become more and more sensitively, more and more lovingly aware of what she has contributed —and what she has become. Each of us has become more fully, more distinctly in my mind, a unique person. But I don't grow in my love so very fast. I still get the two of us confused.

On Love and Trust

At many times it has seemed to me, that to try to discover how to offer and accept love involved fundamental validities more important than validities of knowledge and skill, as important as they are. It has seemed to me that offering love in the form of human support involved being dependable and trustworthy and consistent.

I shall remember for a long time the attempts I made to implement some things I thought I had learned about being helpful by being completely acceptant of another person, dependably and consistently acceptant. I offered warm interest, attention, orientation, and clarification of our thoughts and feelings, but I offered no opinion, no suggestion, no direction. I tried hard to remain much involved and active in our work, and warmly concerned about him, but I also tried hard to say nothing, to do nothing which would imply that I thought what my friend said or did was good or bad or right or wrong.

Sometimes, for limited periods, I was able to do it, to be dependably and consistently and warmly acceptant. My friend really seemed to know that he could expect consistent warmth and acceptance from me. He really seemed to know that I would express no evaluation of him. He knew, and I knew, that I would neither agree nor disagree, neither approve nor disapprove. He could feel clearly and firmly and surely that we would not get involved in the distress that seems almost always to go with the judging of one man by another.

As comfortable and as confident as he was about the nonjudgmental nature of our relationship, my friend was sometimes confused about whether I was helping him—sometimes, about whether I even wanted to help him. Even when he felt he had been helped, he was not sure how I had helped him. Sometimes, he even had trouble fully understanding whether I had any part at all in his thinking and planning about his work.

I remembered Claudia's suitor and I remem-

bered that, if one has been successful in his helping, one's work can become the possession of
another. There really was a sense of loss that
made me sad, and I grieved for the lost sense
of sharing.

Selfishness and reality and mutual support and
reciprocity of emotions were not very clearly
separated out. It seemed to me that really they
needed to be separated out, if he and I were to
be clearly separate individuals. And we continued to work.

The next sense of loss came when my friend
became fully aware that, in our consistently
acceptant relationship, he would never know
where I stood on issues of importance to him.
At some very crucial times he experienced my
nonjudgmental role as evasive and irresponsible.
At those crucial times he felt that I had deprived
him of an important resource, my opinion. He
was pretty sure I held one and he was correct, I
did. But I said to myself that he must learn to
deal with this dependency of his, that I really
could not make his judgments for him. But I
didn't convince myself. He did not really expect
me to make his judgments for him; he just expected me to express my opinions on issues of
crucial importance to him.

There were other times, times while I was suc-
cessfully, dependably, and consistently acceptant, when I found myself acting acceptant even
though I really felt rejecting or annoyed or re-

sentful or hostile. At such times I found myself asking, "Is this being trustworthy?"

It seemed to me that to be trustworthy would mean to try to act just the way I am, to try my best to know myself and to express myself so that I communicate to my fellows, including those I love the most, just what I am, what I think, and how I feel: calm or excited, confident or scared, affectionate or hostile, friendly or cold, acceptant or rejecting.

Being critical and rejecting and hostile is being me, but not completely me. I also love. I have asked myself whether I can develop enough self-awareness and skill to express and communicate all of me at once: the loving and the hating, the helping and the hindering, the criticizing and the supporting, the rebellion and the loyalty, the shifting feelings and the trustworthy intent. Probably not.

I can watch and act and think and slowly learn more about me and you. I can practice and evaluate and slowly learn better to express more nearly all of what I am at any one time. It is just too much to expect, though, that I would ever really learn to do it. To express clearly all of me at once, that is *much* too much. I'm sure that this means that sometimes I won't be helpful. Any person with a problem will find himself provoked to resent me or attack me or resist me or ignore me. I feel pretty sure, though, if he stays with me long enough, he may come to believe that I am trying hard to be dependably and trustworthily and consistently me—and, in time, all of me. In time, I might hope, my friend would come to believe that being as exactly me as I can be is being dependable and consistent and trustworthy and, sometimes, helpful and supportive and affectionate.

The things I do in the face of these conflicts of mine are not so very valid and incisive and precise. I do the best I can. I can sit quietly when I want to speak of my love, if I can believe that my friend can use my silence better than he can use my words. I can express only a part of me at one time, and I can hope that my friend will stick around to learn more of me. I can sometimes be well enough satisfied knowing that some people will never know more than a small part of me. Often the worst part of me.

I guess the most important thing about human beings trying to offer love to one another is that, even at its very best, offering love doesn't necessarily have a happy ending.

On Seeking Love

If it is hard for me to offer love, it is almost impossible to ask for it. Even with the people who love me the most, I find times when I feel as if I could cry for a touch of affection. I feel as if I could, but I don't act as if I could. I say to myself, "What is so hard? They love you. Reach out a hand. They'll take it." That's what I say to myself, but not a move do I make.

I go through the whole routine again, and I

remind myself that love is really simple and can be simply sought. Love is really open and can be openly sought. Love is really happy and can be happily sought. Love is really human and can be humanly sought. I know that love really is all those things and more, but the knowledge doesn't sustain me.

Often, when I have been in need of love, I have found myself wondering how others really feel about me. The need to know sends me to those who love me most, asking "Who am I to you? What are your feelings about me?"

My loved ones know that I am asking for love, and they know I am asking for the stern truth at the same time. The truth is easier to hear from those who love you. They know that I am scared, too, because I really mean what they hear me ask.

They try. They love me and they feel that they must offer me their best efforts at authentic truth and warmest love. There is much that they can say: that they feel happy with me and gently loved, that they feel worried with me and estranged by my moods, that they feel excited with me and charged by my love of life, that they feel angry with me and resentful of my relentless demands, that they feel affectionate toward me and warmed by my love, that they feel afraid for me and concerned about my probings into my being and theirs. It is much to say, and many who love me say it well.

But they know and I know that it is not enough.

They know and I know that I have asked for the impossible. My need for love *is* quieted by what they say—for now. To talk of love is not enough. My need for love is never really quieted very long by words, as true and joyful as they are. My need can be filled only by living in love.

When I raise a hand, or wink an eye, or open an arm, or look with tenderness, or gently touch, I am offering and asking for love. I must learn to look, to listen, to feel, to sense what you do: raise your hand toward me, turn your eyes in a glance of intimacy, open your arms, touch my hand. Love is given in so many ways. In a laundered sock or a fresh shirt, in a warm cup or a cool glass, in a special dish or a special chair, in a proud glance or a worried frown, in a bright smile or a broad grin.

I must watch, I must act, I must watch again and think, only to act again and watch again and think again, in the faith that the cycle will bring both of us closer to the love we seek and closer to the truth about what we do and who we are in the sharing of our life together.

For a long time I was sure that I could not be both lover and observer at the same time. To observe myself and you, I was sure, would kill our love. But as I grew older and more deeply involved in loving, I found that I could be—we could be—both participants and observers all the time, that, indeed, to be both full participant and full observer is the great human talent that sets us all apart from animals without consciousness and enables us to live life twice as richly.

There is a sharp dilemma, though, even as I act and watch, I can't seek love by action and watching in any authentic way until there is a kind of atmosphere, a human climate, that will enable me to act and watch and think, and the climate can't be created unless I act and watch and think. There I stand.

How do I know what to do? I don't. I make a small act on faith—a small provisional try. And then, I watch and listen and feel and think and try to sense what love I can offer and seek with dignity and humility. If I am going to live out my love with others in our day-to-day work and play, with all the complications that such living implies, it seems to me that I have not only a duty first to act on faith but, also, a duty to learn as much as I can about what is going on.

But I can never know all of love. I watch before I act, and I act, and I watch again and try fully to sense and feel. It can be incredibly fast, but it is what I try to do. Sometimes I help create a human climate in which we can be more nearly ourselves in love.

On Intimacy and Commitment

Many people feel that love is an all-or-nothing thing. They feel that to love at all is to love completely, to give completely, to take completely. I don't think that is love. I think that is possession.

In some way, rooted deep in the values of many cultures, to seek love or even to give love is to make a demand. The simplest is the demand for love's return. The deepest and most taxing is the demand for a lasting commitment of mutual support. I would wager that in every culture intimacy entails commitment. The closer the intimacy, the more extensive the commitment. A passing acquaintance may entail no more than a commitment to wish him well when you leave him. A fellow worker is a closer friend than a passing acquaintance, and the commitment is longer lasting and more extensive—to do one's part at work, to share responsibilities for the quality of the product, and to join him at least a little at play. A close friendship entails an even longer and wider commitment—to share his joys and troubles, to help to cope with life's accidents, to stand by in failures, and to celebrate successes. The most intimate of relationships is marriage, and it involves the longest, the most extensive, and the most intensive commitments —to do one's part at family work, to share joys and griefs and successes and failures, to join at open play, and to share the responsibility for the nurture and the quality of the product, the children. Most of the tragedies of extramarital sexual intercourse grow out of the violations of commitments to mutual support in times of trouble, the unstated but almost always unconsciously assumed commitments that go with intimacy. It is remarkably pervasive and deeply instilled, even in the unconscious of the most free and wild, this assumption that intimacy involves commitment.

On Love—Sought and Offered

I have been given my hardest emotional task when a friend of mine has made a serious mistake and behaved incompetently or unjustly or immorally. My friends have been given their hardest emotional task when I have made a serious mistake and behaved incompetently or unjustly or immorally. For me to see, clearly and objectively, just how I was wrong, so that I may learn from my experience, for me to face this moment of pain and truth requires the most creative kind of support.

I need no admonition to "forget it." I need to examine it. To examine it, I need a great deal of compassionate support and a little escapist support. I need no denial of my failure, no pretense that it was a misunderstanding. I need to feel that my fellows are willing to share my failure with me, and, if they were involved in the decision, my punishment with me. I need friends who will continue to express their friendship in public and at the same time rub my nose in my experience in private. I need friends who do not deny me, friends who do help me review and reflect upon and clarify my failure experience. I need friends who are willing to show their faith that I am a man of goodwill and dignity who has made a serious mistake, who is willing to take his share of the punishment, and who can learn from his experience. I need friends who are not afraid to be identified with disgrace.

I have had two very different and very special friends in my time. Each had his own special way of keeping me in touch with the core meaning of being human. One was mentally retarded, they say. His name was Cartwright and we called him Cart. Cart's brain had been injured at birth but his heart had not. Because of the fine sensitivity of his feelings, he had a rare and keen perspective on human affairs. From time to time, he talked to me of his concern about finding a place in life. Once, in the dusk of summer's evening, Cart grew eloquent. I think I shall always remember each word just the way he said it.

"I'm a growed man now. I know that I can't do many things. I can't do many things everybody else can do." He paused to collect his thoughts.

"I had so much trouble remembering my address. I was near growed before I could remember it quick if you asked me. And my Social Security number. I said it over and over for months and months. Now I keep it wrote down. But I'm proud I got one. I got one all my own. I remember that. It means there is something I can do, something I can do good enough to get paid." He stopped again, drew in his breath and let it out in a great sigh.

"I'm thirty years old. I know I am slow. I know that good. Retarded—I know that word. Man, I know that word." He stopped again for a long time. He seemed to be caught up in his thoughts; then, in a burst:

"I'm still ashamed—of that—retarded. I'm sure I ought not to be. No matter what people think, I ought not to be ashamed. Even retarded, there is something I can do. Not just so great, but

something, something worth doing I can do. I
know how to be proud of little things. I know
what it means to love little things. I have been
proud. In school, I was just a boy, but I was
proud—of a picture I painted. Now I am a man.
There has got to be something, something I can
be proud of doing as a man. A little thing. Just
because I am alive and I am me and I know what
it means to be alive and to be me. To be proud
of little things. I have that special—to love making little things." He looked up at the darkening
sky and then turned to me.

"I think there is," his tone was wistful, "something, somewhere, sometime. I think I will know
it, my little thing. Other people may not know it
is for me, but I will. Something for me I can do.
Something to love doing. Something to do
proud. Even for me."

That was Cart. He "had that special." In a world
full of wonders of which he knew so little, he
was for me one of the wonders of the world.
He was fully human.

Matt, my other special friend, was as different
from Cart as a bulldog is different from a wild
flower. He was named for the apostle Matthew,
of all things, and we called him Matt. He was a
sharp and talented black man who had struggled
to free himself from a painful poverty and struggled to win many a throat-cutting battle with the
men who thrive on others' poverty. By the time
he was thirty he had made it. He found business
competition to his liking, he took sweeping risks,

and he owned substantial parts of several small businesses.

Then, one day, on the complaint of a book-keeper, he was shown to have embezzled funds, to have stolen money away from other people. We had been friends a long time, and I tried to stand by firmly during his arrest and arraign-ment. Beside his tough, cool, composure I felt unnecessary, but I stayed until he was free on bail and awaiting trial. After we left the building, by some unspoken consent, we sat a long time in my car. His cool facade melted away, and he spoke with a catch in his voice. I think I will re-member a long time each word he said, too.

"I just found out how greedy I am. I just found out that I really am a dishonest man. Nah, now, it's not a confession. I'm not asking forgiveness and I'm not looking for punishment. I'm looking at my place in life.

"What I have to get straight is that I *am* greedy and dishonest. I didn't even know I was." He paused pensively. "Get what you can. That's the name of the game, and I like the game. The whole world is greedy and dishonest and rough. They're out to get anything I got—people who don't even know me—Sunday school teachers and all. You, too, Jack. You're out to get some-thing from me. At least my friendship, maybe a contact with my life. Maybe I'm your research, your data. I don't know." He paused again to watch my reaction.

"Maybe," I said. "You really are one special kind of contact with life."

"You act friendly, anyway." He said and returned to his thoughts.

"Now I've got caught grabbing. Watch the vultures fly in to pick the bones. I know. I fly with them." He stopped, took his dead cigar out of his mouth, and turned back to me.

"I'm cut down now—not so cool and smart. But I'm not going suddenly to be a new man. I'm not ashamed enough. I don't even think I ought to be ashamed. I never promised anybody to be honest. Not once." He paused again.

"What I am is mixed up. I am. I am very much mixed up about what I am, or where I am. Is there a place in the world for a man who is greedy and dishonest? I mean a real place—no front. In court or out, in jail or out, is there a way to live in peace with myself? Is there something I can do with just a little pride? Even me? Is there a way for a greedy man to be proud of doing something simple, clean, and not much noticed?" He paused and pondered and licked his dry lips.

"I want to be noticed. Yeah, I do. But I don't want ever again to be where I am now. I am in jail in myself before I'm even tried. That's stupid, but that's where I am. The thing is that I don't know where I can be or where I want to be. I just don't know."

Matt could never move me the way Cart could.

Being retarded in moral development is not the same thing as being retarded in mental development. But Matt, in his own way, was limited by his injuries, too.

Supporting him was harder, though, because I could not support his greed and dishonesty and I could not act as if I were free of greed and dishonesty. I thought I had to try to find a way to support his solving his moral problems, perhaps to find a way to live honestly with dishonesty all around us. Maybe it was a matter of just being one person who was not out to get much of what he had except in fair exchange, an exchange of friendship for trust, and to offer him something of my contact with life in exchange for something of his contact with life. I'm pretty sure to support anybody or to love anybody, Cart or Matt or wife or child, is to work out a joint quest for a sensible place in life.

I think again and again about this call for human support, not assistance but support, a very different kind of human support. I wonder again about the whole business of the reciprocity of the interchange of human emotions. I'm pretty sure that compliments, congratulations, promotions, power, and prestige in this world have to be earned somehow by making human investments and taking risks, by competent human work and valid human interchange.

As sure as I am about the reciprocity of these things, I still wonder whether it is just possible that there is a kind of fundamental human support that doesn't require competence or even morality in return. I wonder whether there isn't some basic kind of support to which all of us are entitled just because we are human. Maybe there is a kind of human support that doesn't have to be earned, that is free. All of us humans, the dull and the brilliant, the strong and the weak, the privileged and the deprived, the moral and the immoral, the competent and the incompetent, the loved and the unloved—all of us humans are in this thing together. We can't share equally the praise and the power, but we can share the goodwill, the respect, the faith in the potential of humanity—the faith that every man can, with support, learn from his mistakes and teach us about our mistakes. The tricky task is to provide this kind of support without compromising the reality of the tragic mistakes we make.

I want to suggest that a basic right and a basic duty are involved, a right and a duty that reach deep into consciences of men. I want to suggest that there is a human right to be wrong with dignity. I want to suggest also that there is a reciprocal duty to experiment, a duty to risk failure. Carrying out the human duty to experiment earns one the human right to be wrong, with dignity.

It isn't easy, but it just may be the most important of the emotional problems of living together, and it just may be the investment that will pay the greatest dividends to mankind. It surely requires an unusual marriage of competence and compassion. It surely requires a deep and abiding respect for the never-ending and always fallible human quest for truth and justice and dignity and love.

This human quest, this always fallible and always unfinished human quest, goes far beyond the simple notion that man must cope with the reality of the world around him, as valid as that notion is. This quest reaches deep into the nature of human affairs. It seeks an authentic kind of honor, an honor that can never quail at the truth, however painful, and that can never sacrifice the dignity of a man who, for a time, cannot find the justice, the truth, and the love he seeks.

5
On the Quests:
for Truth, for Justice, for Love

I started out to define the problems—the emotional problems of living with people. I started out just to define the problems, not to solve them. They are perpetual problems. We come round to them again and again, each time getting a little closer or a little farther away from the solutions. The tension rises and then it drops, but it never goes away.

Working on such problems is like having children. It is an act of faith in the future. That faith sustains me.

To ask when to fight and when to run away and how to fight and how to run away is to ask me to consider and reconsider regularly, day after day, how fight and flight are all mixed up with all of human affairs: ambition, both reasonable and unreasonable; respect for human values, both practical and idealistic; work, both creative and compulsive; self-esteem, both vain and humble.

I think that to fight competently and to run away creatively, I need some better basis for foresight than I usually have. I need some firmly agreed-upon mutual expectations and limitations between me and my enemy. I need some kind of Geneva Convention, some Marquis of Queensberry Rules. I need some basis for foresight because I need to calculate risks. I need to be sure about what I am willing to destroy, what can be rebuilt more firmly or more beautifully, what suffering I am willing to inflict, how deep a wound must be before I stop jabbing.

On the Quests: for Truth, for Justice, for Love

But I, or my enemies and I, must make the rules as we go, while the fights and the flights go on.
Am I willing to destroy a man's house, however battered and shabby? He invested his sweat in it, and to destroy it is to destroy a part of him. Am I willing to destroy a school, however oppressive and grim? Somebody learned to cope with his world in it, with his teachers or against them. Am I willing to destroy a hospital, however inhuman and stinking? Somebody found relief from his pain in it. Am I willing to destroy a painting, however stilted or confusing? Somebody found new spirit in it. A person, however immoral and evil? He found a life he didn't ask for, and it turned out to be the only important thing to him. A baby, however small and insignificant? Each one is a hope made visible, and without hope there is nothing.

There are all kinds of fights and all kinds of flights, and each needs some special basis for foresight. There are the times for fight and the times for flight. A quick fight is an urge to hurt in revenge; a quick, short flight can temper the urge. A time of righteous anger is a driving feeling of outrage; a little sensible flight can turn the feeling into a sense of honor, an emotion that can sustain me to be sure that I fight for what I really believe in. A quick, courageous fight is one basis of self-respect; a quick, prudent flight is one basis of self-preservation.

There are ways to fight and ways to run away. A competent fight is a sharp skill at destruction, fast, strong, and clear; a creative flight can transform the competence into skills at timing, cycling, negotiation, humanely limiting the destruction. A fight of self-appraisal is really necessary if I am to see clearly the true nature of the products of my work; some reflective flight can give me the perspective and the strength to look unflinchingly at the outcomes of what I have done.

Fight is a part of life; flight is a part of life. I need both to judge whether my life is really a faltering and fallible, but honest and open, struggle for human dignity and freedom or just another greedy fight for vainglory and domination.

The critical problems of forming a basis for foresight to guide my fights and flights are problems of finding the real nature of my world and myself; the struggle lies at the mainspring of the never-ending human quest for truth.

Dependency and dependability are inseparable parts of living with others. As long as I live with other people, I find myself dependent and I find myself dependable, whether I mean to be or not. Each day I change and the world changes. I find myself changing my ideas and feelings about realistic dependencies and dependabilities and about a fair price to pay for the resources they bring to me.

There are some resources I must develop for myself, partly because I need them to be available to me unconditionally, anywhere, anytime (such as stamina), and partly because I need them for my self-respect (such as courage). Some resources I must depend upon others to supply for me, partly because I cannot supply them so well for myself (such as surgical skill) and partly because I like others to do some things for me (such as making great music). But my feelings about reciprocity run deep within me. I cannot live very long in debt and be at peace with myself. Some resources I must supply for others, partly because they could not supply them so well for themselves (such as studying and reflecting) and partly because I like to do some things for others (such as listening to them). I must keep asking myself questions, as I change and the world changes, about what is a fair interchange.

Dependency has vulnerability in it and dependency has strength in it. It has vulnerability in it because I must trust others to be dependable. It has strength in it because it gives me resources I could never have alone. I am pretty sure that freedom and significance require dependency and dependability. Freedom is being dependent upon people who are dependable to me, at a fair price. Significance is being dependable to people who are dependent on me, at a fair price. Without both freedom and significance, without both dependency and dependability, I think, there is no just or lasting power or peace among men who must live together.

I must keep asking myself questions about what

is just and lasting. How I answer them will be determined in part by a slow-working, but enormously powerful, way of seeking spoken and unspoken agreements with one another about what is a fair interchange of our resources: what we will require of those on whom we depend and what we will provide to those who depend upon us. The questions of when to be dependent and when to be dependable and how to be dependent and how to be dependable are at the very core of the never-ending human quest for justice.

To ask when to offer love and when to seek love and how to offer love and how to seek love is to unfold the great human tragedy. The one human resource so much needed by all of us is the one human resource that gets the most confused expression and the most cautious acceptance. The one great human resource for which nearly all of us are starving is also the one resource that I find so frighteningly exposing of old wounds, so often fearfully pushed back inside me, so tangled with little knots of feeling, and so often blurted out in anguish. It is so clumsy and fragmented and awkward in its expression; it is so graceful and warm and tender in its nature.

Strong men, tough and real, are lovers, too, tender and warm inside. Cool women, poised and composed, are lovers, too, soft and glowing inside. All those surges of human light and joy come through clearly only on rare, private, and protected times. And those times are remembered forever. There is so much inside, so much light and joy that is so badly needed, but so little ever gets out, so pitifully little ever gets out into the stream of human interchange.

Twice in my life I thought it possible that I was about to die. Both times the prospect compelled me to seek what I have left undone. Both times I knew that I had failed to find a way to show my love; both times I knew that those I loved most would never really feel and know how much, how tenderly, how deeply I loved them. Should I die today, it would be the same. I still have not found a way to let my loved ones know how much I love them. That is the great tragedy of the life I live.

Perhaps I must get farther along toward knowing what I am doing in my fights and flights, dependencies and dependabilities, before I can find freedom for my love. But I cannot wait for that. To free my love now is to seek some basic essence, some bone marrow of human support that doesn't have to be earned. It is to seek some form of love to which all of us are entitled just because we are human and alive. To turn the trick is to chase those fleeting wisps of glory when, without one whit of concern about rejection, without one thought about duties to respond, without one glance at equities in exchange, without anything but the zest in the expression, I can love and be loved as freely, as openly, as joyfully, and as confidently as can be.

It is a rare jewel and a great event, and it really is at the core of the never-ending quest for love.

These, then, were the problems I started out to define:

When to fight and when to run away and how to fight and how to run away and

When to be dependent and when to be dependable and how to be dependent and how to be dependable and

When to offer love and when to seek love and how to offer love and how to seek love.

And the problems have become never-ending quests: the human quest for truth, the human quest for justice, and the human quest for love.

I shall continue to follow these never-ending quests with zest and fatigue, with courage and fear, with painful fallacies and joyful insights. I hope my children will continue the never-ending quests, too, for if they stop, they will finally have lost faith in the future, and that will make them sterile and that will be the end of mankind.